50 Southern BBQ and Grill Masterclass Recipes for Home

By: Kelly Johnson

Table of Contents

- Classic Southern BBQ Ribs
- Pulled Pork Sandwiches with Tangy BBQ Sauce
- Smoked Brisket with Bourbon BBQ Glaze
- BBQ Chicken Wings with Honey-Sriracha Sauce
- Grilled Shrimp Skewers with Cajun Seasoning
- Texas-Style Smoked Beef Brisket
- Memphis Dry Rub Ribs
- Carolina-style Pulled Pork Sandwiches with Vinegar-based BBQ Sauce
- Smoked Turkey Legs with Spicy Peach BBQ Sauce
- BBQ Bacon-Wrapped Shrimp
- Alabama White BBQ Chicken
- Kansas City-Style Burnt Ends
- Bourbon-Marinated Grilled Steak
- Southern BBQ Chicken Drumsticks
- Smoked Sausage with Sweet and Spicy BBQ Sauce
- BBQ Pulled Chicken Sliders with Coleslaw
- Grilled Corn on the Cob with Chili Lime Butter
- Southern-Style BBQ Baked Beans
- BBQ Pork Belly Burnt Ends
- Carolina Mustard BBQ Sauce
- Classic Southern Potato Salad
- Grilled Sweet Tea-Brined Chicken
- Texas BBQ Beef Ribs
- Smoked Mac and Cheese
- Grilled Peach and Bourbon BBQ Pork Chops
- Spicy Cajun BBQ Shrimp Po' Boys
- Smoked Pork Shoulder with Carolina Vinegar Sauce
- Alabama BBQ Chicken Sliders with White BBQ Sauce
- BBQ Pulled Chicken Nachos
- Southern BBQ Spare Ribs
- Grilled Watermelon Salad with Feta and Mint
- Smoked Cornbread with Honey Butter
- BBQ Bacon-Wrapped Jalapeno Poppers
- Memphis-Style BBQ Pulled Pork Sandwiches
- Texas BBQ Chili

- Bourbon BBQ Glazed Salmon
- Southern Coleslaw with Tangy Dressing
- Grilled Okra with Cajun Seasoning
- BBQ Chicken and Pineapple Skewers
- Nashville Hot Chicken Sandwiches
- Smoked Beef Short Ribs
- Sweet Potato Casserole with Pecan Streusel Topping
- Cajun BBQ Shrimp and Grits
- Grilled Asparagus with Lemon-Herb Butter
- BBQ Pulled Pork Stuffed Sweet Potatoes
- Smoked Chicken Thighs with Alabama White Sauce
- Southern BBQ Baked Macaroni and Cheese
- Grilled Artichokes with Garlic-Herb Butter
- Bourbon BBQ Glazed Pork Tenderloin
- BBQ Pulled Jackfruit Sandwiches (for a vegetarian option)

Classic Southern BBQ Ribs

Ingredients:

- 2 racks of pork baby back ribs (about 4-5 pounds total)
- 1/4 cup brown sugar
- 2 tablespoons paprika
- 1 tablespoon garlic powder
- 1 tablespoon onion powder
- 1 tablespoon chili powder
- 1 tablespoon ground cumin
- 1 tablespoon salt
- 1 tablespoon black pepper
- 1 cup barbecue sauce (your favorite store-bought or homemade)

Instructions:

Preheat your grill to medium heat, around 250-275°F (120-135°C). If using a charcoal grill, set it up for indirect heat by placing the coals on one side of the grill.

Prepare the ribs by removing the membrane from the back of the racks. Use a paper towel to grip and pull off the membrane for easier removal.

In a small bowl, mix together the brown sugar, paprika, garlic powder, onion powder, chili powder, cumin, salt, and black pepper to make the dry rub.

Rub the dry rub mixture evenly over both sides of the ribs, pressing gently to adhere.

Place the ribs on the grill, bone-side down, over indirect heat. Close the lid and let them cook for about 2-3 hours, or until the meat is tender and starts to pull away from the bones. Maintain the grill temperature around 250-275°F (120-135°C) throughout the cooking process.

During the last 30 minutes of cooking, brush the ribs with barbecue sauce, turning and brushing occasionally to build up a flavorful glaze.

Once the ribs are tender and glazed, remove them from the grill and let them rest for a few minutes before serving.

Slice the ribs between the bones and serve hot, with extra barbecue sauce on the side if desired.

Enjoy your classic Southern BBQ ribs with your favorite sides like coleslaw, cornbread, baked beans, or potato salad. They're perfect for a backyard barbecue or any occasion when you're craving delicious, fall-off-the-bone ribs!

Pulled Pork Sandwiches with Tangy BBQ Sauce

Ingredients:

For the Pulled Pork:

- 4-5 pounds pork shoulder (also known as pork butt), boneless
- 2 tablespoons brown sugar
- 2 tablespoons paprika
- 2 tablespoons garlic powder
- 2 tablespoons onion powder
- 1 tablespoon chili powder
- 1 tablespoon ground cumin
- 1 tablespoon salt
- 1 tablespoon black pepper
- 1 cup chicken or vegetable broth
- 1 cup apple cider vinegar
- 1 cup barbecue sauce (for serving)

For the Tangy BBQ Sauce:

- 1 cup ketchup
- 1/2 cup apple cider vinegar
- 1/4 cup brown sugar
- 2 tablespoons Worcestershire sauce
- 1 tablespoon Dijon mustard
- 1 teaspoon garlic powder
- 1 teaspoon onion powder
- Salt and pepper to taste

For Serving:

- Hamburger buns or sandwich rolls
- Coleslaw (optional, for topping)

Instructions:

1. Prepare the Pulled Pork:

    In a small bowl, mix together the brown sugar, paprika, garlic powder, onion powder, chili powder, cumin, salt, and black pepper to make the dry rub.

Rub the dry rub mixture evenly over the pork shoulder, covering all sides. Let it sit at room temperature for about 30 minutes to allow the flavors to penetrate. Preheat your oven to 300°F (150°C).

Place the seasoned pork shoulder in a roasting pan or Dutch oven. Pour the chicken or vegetable broth and apple cider vinegar over the pork.

Cover the roasting pan or Dutch oven with aluminum foil or a lid and roast in the preheated oven for 6-8 hours, or until the pork is very tender and easily shreds with a fork.

Once the pork is cooked, remove it from the oven and let it cool slightly. Use two forks to shred the meat into bite-sized pieces, discarding any large pieces of fat.

Drain excess liquid from the pan, then mix the shredded pork with your favorite barbecue sauce to coat. Keep warm until ready to serve.

2. Prepare the Tangy BBQ Sauce:

In a small saucepan, combine the ketchup, apple cider vinegar, brown sugar, Worcestershire sauce, Dijon mustard, garlic powder, and onion powder.

Bring the mixture to a simmer over medium heat, stirring occasionally.

Let the sauce simmer for about 10-15 minutes, or until it thickens slightly.

Season with salt and pepper to taste. Remove from heat and let cool slightly before serving.

3. Assemble the Pulled Pork Sandwiches:

Toast the hamburger buns or sandwich rolls if desired.

Spoon a generous amount of the pulled pork onto the bottom half of each bun.

Top the pulled pork with a dollop of tangy BBQ sauce.

If desired, add a scoop of coleslaw on top of the BBQ sauce.

Place the top half of the bun on top to complete the sandwich.

Serve immediately, with extra BBQ sauce on the side for dipping or drizzling.

Enjoy your delicious pulled pork sandwiches with tangy BBQ sauce! They're perfect for a backyard barbecue, game day, or any casual gathering with friends and family.

Smoked Brisket with Bourbon BBQ Glaze

Ingredients:

For the Brisket:

- 1 whole beef brisket (about 10-12 pounds), preferably untrimmed
- 1/4 cup kosher salt
- 1/4 cup coarsely ground black pepper
- 2 tablespoons paprika
- 2 tablespoons garlic powder
- 2 tablespoons onion powder
- Wood chips or chunks for smoking (hickory, oak, or mesquite)

For the Bourbon BBQ Glaze:

- 1 cup ketchup
- 1/2 cup bourbon whiskey
- 1/4 cup apple cider vinegar
- 1/4 cup brown sugar
- 2 tablespoons Worcestershire sauce
- 1 tablespoon Dijon mustard
- 1 tablespoon molasses
- 1 teaspoon garlic powder
- 1 teaspoon onion powder
- 1/2 teaspoon smoked paprika
- Salt and pepper to taste

Instructions:

1. Prepare the Brisket:

   Trim any excess fat from the surface of the brisket, leaving a thin layer (about 1/4 inch) to keep the meat moist during smoking.
   In a small bowl, combine the kosher salt, black pepper, paprika, garlic powder, and onion powder to make the dry rub.
   Rub the dry rub mixture evenly over the surface of the brisket, covering all sides.
   Let the brisket sit at room temperature for about 1 hour to allow the flavors to penetrate.

2. Preheat the Smoker:

Meanwhile, prepare your smoker according to manufacturer's instructions and preheat it to a temperature of 225-250°F (107-121°C). Use your choice of wood chips or chunks for smoking (hickory, oak, or mesquite work well with brisket).

3. Smoke the Brisket:

Place the seasoned brisket on the smoker grate, fat side up.
Close the lid and let the brisket smoke for several hours, maintaining a consistent temperature of 225-250°F (107-121°C). Plan for about 1 to 1 1/2 hours of smoking time per pound of brisket.
After the initial smoking period, you can periodically check the internal temperature of the brisket using a meat thermometer. The brisket is ready to be glazed when the internal temperature reaches around 160-165°F (71-74°C).

4. Make the Bourbon BBQ Glaze:

In a saucepan over medium heat, combine the ketchup, bourbon whiskey, apple cider vinegar, brown sugar, Worcestershire sauce, Dijon mustard, molasses, garlic powder, onion powder, and smoked paprika.
Bring the mixture to a simmer, then reduce the heat to low and let it simmer gently for about 15-20 minutes, stirring occasionally, until the sauce thickens slightly.
Season the sauce with salt and pepper to taste. Remove from heat and set aside.

5. Glaze the Brisket:

Once the brisket reaches an internal temperature of around 160-165°F (71-74°C), brush a generous amount of the bourbon BBQ glaze over the surface of the brisket.
Continue to smoke the brisket, brushing on additional glaze every 30 minutes or so, until the internal temperature reaches 195-205°F (90-96°C) and the meat is tender and fully cooked.

6. Rest and Serve:

Remove the smoked brisket from the smoker and transfer it to a cutting board. Tent the brisket loosely with aluminum foil and let it rest for about 30 minutes to allow the juices to redistribute.
Slice the brisket against the grain into thin slices. Serve the smoked brisket with the remaining bourbon BBQ glaze on the side.

Enjoy your delicious smoked brisket with bourbon BBQ glaze! It's sure to be a hit at your next barbecue or special gathering.

BBQ Chicken Wings with Honey-Sriracha Sauce

Ingredients:

For the Chicken Wings:

- 2 pounds chicken wings, split into flats and drumettes
- 2 tablespoons olive oil
- Salt and pepper to taste
- 1 teaspoon garlic powder
- 1 teaspoon onion powder
- 1 teaspoon paprika
- 1/2 teaspoon cayenne pepper (optional, for extra heat)

For the Honey-Sriracha Sauce:

- 1/4 cup sriracha sauce
- 1/4 cup honey
- 2 tablespoons soy sauce
- 2 tablespoons rice vinegar
- 2 cloves garlic, minced
- 1 teaspoon grated ginger
- 1 tablespoon sesame oil
- Sesame seeds and chopped green onions for garnish (optional)

Instructions:

1. Prepare the Chicken Wings:

> Preheat your oven to 400°F (200°C). Line a baking sheet with aluminum foil and place a wire rack on top.
> In a large bowl, toss the chicken wings with olive oil, salt, pepper, garlic powder, onion powder, paprika, and cayenne pepper (if using) until evenly coated.
> Arrange the seasoned chicken wings on the prepared wire rack in a single layer, leaving space between each wing.
> Bake in the preheated oven for 40-45 minutes, flipping halfway through, or until the wings are golden brown and crispy.

2. Make the Honey-Sriracha Sauce:

In a small saucepan, combine the sriracha sauce, honey, soy sauce, rice vinegar, minced garlic, and grated ginger.
Bring the mixture to a simmer over medium heat, stirring occasionally.
Let the sauce simmer for about 5-7 minutes, or until it thickens slightly.
Remove the saucepan from the heat and stir in the sesame oil.

3. Coat the Chicken Wings:

Once the chicken wings are cooked and crispy, transfer them to a large bowl.
Pour the honey-sriracha sauce over the wings and toss until evenly coated.

4. Serve:

Transfer the glazed chicken wings to a serving platter.
Garnish with sesame seeds and chopped green onions if desired.
Serve immediately, and enjoy your delicious BBQ chicken wings with honey-sriracha sauce!

These wings are perfect for serving as a party appetizer, game day snack, or as part of a casual meal. They're sure to be a crowd-pleaser with their irresistible combination of sweet and spicy flavors.

Grilled Shrimp Skewers with Cajun Seasoning

Ingredients:

- 1 pound large shrimp, peeled and deveined
- 2 tablespoons olive oil
- 2 cloves garlic, minced
- 1 tablespoon Cajun seasoning (store-bought or homemade)
- 1/2 teaspoon paprika
- 1/4 teaspoon cayenne pepper (adjust to taste)
- 1/2 teaspoon dried thyme
- 1/2 teaspoon dried oregano
- 1/2 teaspoon salt
- 1/4 teaspoon black pepper
- Juice of 1/2 lemon
- Wooden or metal skewers, soaked in water if wooden

Instructions:

If using wooden skewers, soak them in water for at least 30 minutes to prevent them from burning on the grill.

In a large bowl, combine the olive oil, minced garlic, Cajun seasoning, paprika, cayenne pepper, dried thyme, dried oregano, salt, black pepper, and lemon juice. Mix well to make the marinade.

Add the peeled and deveined shrimp to the bowl with the marinade. Toss to coat the shrimp evenly with the seasoning mixture. Cover the bowl and let the shrimp marinate in the refrigerator for at least 30 minutes, or up to 2 hours for maximum flavor.

Preheat your grill to medium-high heat (around 375-400°F or 190-200°C).

Thread the marinated shrimp onto the skewers, making sure to leave a little space between each shrimp.

Once the grill is hot, place the shrimp skewers directly on the grill grates. Cook for 2-3 minutes per side, or until the shrimp are pink and opaque, and have grill marks.

Remove the shrimp skewers from the grill and transfer them to a serving platter. Garnish with fresh chopped parsley or cilantro if desired.

Serve the grilled shrimp skewers with Cajun seasoning hot, with your favorite sides such as rice, grilled vegetables, or a fresh salad.

Enjoy your delicious grilled shrimp skewers with Cajun seasoning! They're perfect for summer cookouts, backyard BBQs, or any occasion when you want to enjoy tasty grilled seafood.

Texas-Style Smoked Beef Brisket

Ingredients:

- 1 whole beef brisket, preferably untrimmed (about 10-12 pounds)
- Salt and black pepper, to taste
- 1/4 cup paprika
- 1/4 cup brown sugar
- 2 tablespoons garlic powder
- 2 tablespoons onion powder
- 2 tablespoons chili powder
- 1 tablespoon ground cumin
- 1 tablespoon mustard powder
- 1 tablespoon cayenne pepper (adjust to taste)
- Wood chips or chunks for smoking (hickory or oak work well)

Instructions:

1. Prepare the Brisket:

   Trim any excess fat from the surface of the brisket, leaving a thin layer (about 1/4 inch) to keep the meat moist during smoking.

   In a small bowl, combine the paprika, brown sugar, garlic powder, onion powder, chili powder, cumin, mustard powder, cayenne pepper, salt, and black pepper to make the dry rub.

   Season the brisket generously on all sides with the dry rub mixture, pressing it into the meat to adhere. Let the brisket sit at room temperature for about 1 hour to allow the flavors to penetrate.

2. Preheat the Smoker:

   Meanwhile, prepare your smoker according to manufacturer's instructions and preheat it to a temperature of 225-250°F (107-121°C). Use your choice of wood chips or chunks for smoking (hickory or oak work well with brisket).

3. Smoke the Brisket:

   Place the seasoned brisket on the smoker grate, fat side up.

   Close the lid and let the brisket smoke for several hours, maintaining a consistent temperature of 225-250°F (107-121°C). Plan for about 1 to 1 1/2 hours of smoking time per pound of brisket.

After the initial smoking period, you can periodically check the internal temperature of the brisket using a meat thermometer. The brisket is ready to be wrapped in foil (or butcher paper) when it reaches around 160-165°F (71-74°C).

4. Wrap the Brisket:

　　Once the brisket reaches the desired temperature, remove it from the smoker.
　　Wrap the brisket tightly in aluminum foil (or butcher paper) to help it retain moisture and continue cooking.
　　Place the wrapped brisket back on the smoker and continue cooking until it reaches an internal temperature of 195-205°F (90-96°C). This can take several more hours, depending on the size of the brisket.

5. Rest and Serve:

　　Once the brisket is fully cooked and tender, remove it from the smoker and let it rest, wrapped in foil, for at least 30 minutes to 1 hour.
　　Carefully unwrap the brisket and transfer it to a cutting board.
　　Slice the brisket against the grain into thin slices.
　　Serve the Texas-style smoked beef brisket hot, with your favorite barbecue sauce or alongside traditional sides like coleslaw, baked beans, and cornbread.

Enjoy your delicious Texas-style smoked beef brisket! It's sure to be a hit at your next barbecue or special gathering.

Memphis Dry Rub Ribs

Ingredients:

For the Dry Rub:

- 1/4 cup brown sugar
- 2 tablespoons paprika
- 1 tablespoon garlic powder
- 1 tablespoon onion powder
- 1 tablespoon chili powder
- 1 tablespoon ground black pepper
- 1 tablespoon kosher salt
- 1 teaspoon cayenne pepper (adjust to taste)

For the Ribs:

- 2 racks of pork spare ribs or baby back ribs (about 4-5 pounds total)
- Yellow mustard (optional, for adhering the rub)

Instructions:

1. Prepare the Dry Rub:

    In a small bowl, combine the brown sugar, paprika, garlic powder, onion powder, chili powder, black pepper, salt, and cayenne pepper. Mix well to ensure even distribution of spices.

2. Prepare the Ribs:

    If desired, remove the membrane from the back of the ribs for better flavor penetration. Use a knife to loosen one corner of the membrane, then grip it with a paper towel and peel it off.
    Pat the ribs dry with paper towels.
    Optionally, spread a thin layer of yellow mustard over the ribs. This helps the dry rub adhere to the meat, but it's optional if you prefer not to use it.

3. Apply the Dry Rub:

    Sprinkle the dry rub generously over both sides of the ribs, pressing it into the meat to adhere. Use as much or as little of the rub as you like, depending on your taste preferences.

Let the ribs sit at room temperature for about 30 minutes to allow the flavors to penetrate the meat.

4. Preheat the Grill or Smoker:

    Prepare your grill or smoker for indirect cooking at a temperature of 225-250°F (107-121°C). If using a charcoal grill, set it up for indirect heat by placing the coals on one side of the grill.

5. Smoke the Ribs:

    Once the grill or smoker is preheated, place the ribs on the grate, bone-side down, away from direct heat.
    Close the lid and let the ribs smoke for 3-4 hours, maintaining a consistent temperature of 225-250°F (107-121°C). You can add wood chips or chunks for additional smoke flavor, if desired.

6. Check for Doneness:

    After 3-4 hours of smoking, check the ribs for doneness. They should be tender and have a nice crust on the outside.
    If the ribs are not quite done, continue cooking for another 30 minutes to 1 hour, checking periodically until they reach the desired level of tenderness.

7. Rest and Serve:

    Once the ribs are done, remove them from the grill or smoker and let them rest for a few minutes.
    Slice the ribs between the bones and serve hot, with your favorite barbecue sauce on the side if desired. Enjoy your delicious Memphis dry rub ribs!

These ribs are perfect for a backyard barbecue or any occasion when you want to impress your guests with flavorful and tender barbecue.

Carolina-style Pulled Pork Sandwiches with Vinegar-based BBQ Sauce

Ingredients:

For the Pulled Pork:

- 4-5 pounds pork shoulder (also known as pork butt)
- Salt and black pepper, to taste
- 1 tablespoon brown sugar
- 1 tablespoon paprika
- 1 tablespoon garlic powder
- 1 tablespoon onion powder
- 1 tablespoon mustard powder
- 1/2 teaspoon cayenne pepper (adjust to taste)
- Vinegar-based BBQ sauce (recipe follows)
- Hamburger buns or sandwich rolls, for serving

For the Vinegar-based BBQ Sauce:

- 1 cup apple cider vinegar
- 1/2 cup ketchup
- 1/4 cup brown sugar
- 2 tablespoons yellow mustard
- 1 tablespoon Worcestershire sauce
- 1 teaspoon hot sauce (such as Tabasco)
- 1 teaspoon garlic powder
- 1 teaspoon onion powder
- 1/2 teaspoon black pepper
- Salt to taste

Instructions:

1. Prepare the Pulled Pork:

> In a small bowl, mix together the brown sugar, paprika, garlic powder, onion powder, mustard powder, cayenne pepper, salt, and black pepper to make the dry rub.
> Rub the dry rub mixture evenly over the surface of the pork shoulder, covering all sides. Let the pork shoulder sit at room temperature for about 30 minutes to allow the flavors to penetrate.
> Preheat your oven to 300°F (150°C).

Place the seasoned pork shoulder in a roasting pan or Dutch oven. Cover the pan tightly with aluminum foil or a lid.

Roast the pork shoulder in the preheated oven for 6-8 hours, or until the meat is very tender and easily shreds with a fork.

Once the pork shoulder is cooked, remove it from the oven and let it cool slightly. Use two forks to shred the meat into bite-sized pieces, discarding any large pieces of fat.

Toss the shredded pork with the vinegar-based BBQ sauce (recipe follows) to coat. Keep warm until ready to serve.

2. Make the Vinegar-based BBQ Sauce:

In a medium saucepan, combine the apple cider vinegar, ketchup, brown sugar, yellow mustard, Worcestershire sauce, hot sauce, garlic powder, onion powder, black pepper, and salt.

Bring the mixture to a simmer over medium heat, stirring occasionally.

Let the sauce simmer for about 10-15 minutes, or until it thickens slightly.

Taste and adjust the seasoning, adding more salt or hot sauce if desired.

3. Assemble the Pulled Pork Sandwiches:

Toast the hamburger buns or sandwich rolls if desired.

Spoon a generous amount of the pulled pork onto the bottom half of each bun.

Top the pulled pork with a dollop of vinegar-based BBQ sauce.

Place the top half of the bun on top to complete the sandwich.

Serve immediately, and enjoy your delicious Carolina-style pulled pork sandwiches with vinegar-based BBQ sauce!

These sandwiches are perfect for a casual meal, backyard barbecue, or any occasion when you want to enjoy classic Southern flavors.

Smoked Turkey Legs with Spicy Peach BBQ Sauce

Ingredients:

For the Smoked Turkey Legs:

- 4 turkey legs
- Olive oil
- Salt and pepper to taste
- Your choice of poultry seasoning or dry rub (optional)

For the Spicy Peach BBQ Sauce:

- 2 cups diced peaches (fresh or canned)
- 1/2 cup ketchup
- 1/4 cup apple cider vinegar
- 1/4 cup brown sugar
- 2 tablespoons Worcestershire sauce
- 1 tablespoon Dijon mustard
- 1 teaspoon hot sauce (adjust to taste)
- 1 teaspoon garlic powder
- 1 teaspoon onion powder
- Salt and pepper to taste

Instructions:

1. Prepare the Smoked Turkey Legs:

    Rinse the turkey legs under cold water and pat them dry with paper towels.
    Rub the turkey legs with olive oil and season them generously with salt, pepper, and your choice of poultry seasoning or dry rub. Let them sit at room temperature for about 30 minutes while you prepare the smoker.

2. Preheat the Smoker:

    Prepare your smoker according to manufacturer's instructions and preheat it to a temperature of 225-250°F (107-121°C). Use your choice of wood chips or chunks for smoking (hickory or applewood work well with poultry).

3. Smoke the Turkey Legs:

    Once the smoker is preheated, place the seasoned turkey legs on the smoker grate, making sure they are not touching each other.

Close the lid and let the turkey legs smoke for 3-4 hours, or until they reach an internal temperature of 165°F (74°C) when measured with a meat thermometer.

During the smoking process, periodically check the smoker temperature and add more wood chips or chunks as needed to maintain a steady temperature and smoke level.

4. Make the Spicy Peach BBQ Sauce:

In a saucepan, combine the diced peaches, ketchup, apple cider vinegar, brown sugar, Worcestershire sauce, Dijon mustard, hot sauce, garlic powder, and onion powder.

Bring the mixture to a simmer over medium heat, stirring occasionally.

Let the sauce simmer for about 15-20 minutes, or until the peaches are soft and the sauce has thickened slightly.

Season the sauce with salt and pepper to taste. Remove from heat and set aside.

5. Glaze the Turkey Legs:

Once the turkey legs are fully cooked and reach an internal temperature of 165°F (74°C), brush them generously with the spicy peach BBQ sauce.

Continue to smoke the turkey legs for an additional 15-20 minutes, brushing on more sauce every 5 minutes or so, until the sauce forms a sticky glaze on the outside of the turkey legs.

6. Serve:

Remove the smoked turkey legs from the smoker and transfer them to a serving platter.

Serve hot, with extra spicy peach BBQ sauce on the side for dipping or drizzling.

Enjoy your delicious smoked turkey legs with spicy peach BBQ sauce! They're perfect for a backyard barbecue or any occasion when you want to impress your guests with flavorful and tender smoked meat.

BBQ Bacon-Wrapped Shrimp

Ingredients:

- 1 pound large shrimp, peeled and deveined
- 12 slices of bacon, cut in half
- 1/2 cup barbecue sauce (your favorite store-bought or homemade)
- Wooden toothpicks or metal skewers

Instructions:

Preheat your grill to medium-high heat, around 375-400°F (190-200°C). If using wooden toothpicks, soak them in water for 30 minutes to prevent burning.
Season the shrimp with salt and pepper, if desired.
Take each shrimp and wrap it with a half slice of bacon, securing it with a toothpick or skewer. Repeat with the remaining shrimp and bacon.
Place the bacon-wrapped shrimp on the preheated grill, directly over the heat.
Grill the shrimp for 2-3 minutes on each side, or until the bacon is crispy and the shrimp are pink and opaque.
During the last minute of grilling, brush the shrimp with barbecue sauce on both sides, allowing it to caramelize and form a sticky glaze.
Once the bacon is crispy and the shrimp are cooked through, remove them from the grill and transfer to a serving platter.
Serve the BBQ bacon-wrapped shrimp hot, with extra barbecue sauce on the side for dipping.
Enjoy your delicious BBQ bacon-wrapped shrimp as an appetizer or main dish! They're perfect for a backyard barbecue, game day snack, or any occasion when you want to impress your guests with flavorful and savory shrimp wrapped in crispy bacon.

Alabama White BBQ Chicken

Ingredients:

For the Chicken:

- 4 bone-in, skin-on chicken breasts or thighs
- Salt and black pepper, to taste
- Olive oil, for brushing

For the Alabama White BBQ Sauce:

- 1 cup mayonnaise
- 1/4 cup apple cider vinegar
- 1 tablespoon prepared horseradish
- 1 tablespoon Dijon mustard
- 1 tablespoon lemon juice
- 1 teaspoon granulated sugar
- 1 teaspoon garlic powder
- 1 teaspoon onion powder
- 1/2 teaspoon smoked paprika
- Salt and black pepper, to taste

Instructions:

1. Prepare the Chicken:

    Preheat your grill to medium-high heat, around 375-400°F (190-200°C).
    Season the chicken breasts or thighs generously with salt and black pepper on both sides.
    Brush the chicken with olive oil to prevent sticking and promote browning on the grill.

2. Grill the Chicken:

    Place the seasoned chicken directly on the grill grates, skin-side down, and grill for about 6-8 minutes per side, or until the internal temperature reaches 165°F (74°C) for chicken breasts or 175°F (80°C) for thighs.
    During the last few minutes of grilling, you can brush the chicken with some of the Alabama White BBQ Sauce to add flavor and moisture. Reserve the remaining sauce for serving.
    Once the chicken is fully cooked and has reached the desired level of char and grill marks, remove it from the grill and transfer it to a serving platter.

3. Make the Alabama White BBQ Sauce:

   In a medium bowl, whisk together the mayonnaise, apple cider vinegar, horseradish, Dijon mustard, lemon juice, granulated sugar, garlic powder, onion powder, smoked paprika, salt, and black pepper until smooth and well combined.
   Taste the sauce and adjust the seasoning, adding more salt, pepper, or other ingredients as needed to suit your preferences.

4. Serve:

   Serve the grilled chicken hot, with the Alabama White BBQ Sauce drizzled over the top or served on the side for dipping.
   Optionally, garnish with fresh chopped parsley or chives for a pop of color and freshness.
   Enjoy your delicious Alabama White BBQ Chicken with its tangy and creamy sauce, perfect for a summer barbecue or any occasion!

Kansas City-Style Burnt Ends

Ingredients:

- 3-4 pounds beef brisket point (also known as the fatty end of the brisket)
- Your favorite barbecue rub or seasoning
- BBQ sauce (homemade or store-bought)
- Butter or beef tallow (optional, for added richness)

Instructions:

1. Prepare the Brisket Point:

   Preheat your smoker to 250°F (120°C) using your choice of wood chips or chunks for smoking (hickory, oak, or pecan are traditional choices).
   Trim any excess fat from the surface of the brisket point, leaving about 1/4 inch of fat to render and add flavor during smoking.
   Season the brisket point generously with your favorite barbecue rub or seasoning, covering all sides. Pat the seasoning into the meat to ensure it adheres.

2. Smoke the Brisket Point:

   Place the seasoned brisket point directly on the smoker grate, fat side up.
   Close the lid and smoke the brisket point for about 4-6 hours, or until it reaches an internal temperature of 160°F (71°C).
   Once the brisket point reaches 160°F (71°C), remove it from the smoker and wrap it tightly in aluminum foil to prevent it from drying out. If desired, you can add a few pats of butter or beef tallow to the foil-wrapped brisket point for added richness.
   Return the wrapped brisket point to the smoker and continue cooking until it reaches an internal temperature of 200-205°F (93-96°C). This can take an additional 2-3 hours, depending on the size of the brisket point.

3. Cube and Sauce the Burnt Ends:

   Once the brisket point reaches 200-205°F (93-96°C), remove it from the smoker and let it rest in the foil for about 30 minutes to allow the juices to redistribute.
   Unwrap the brisket point and transfer it to a cutting board. Use a sharp knife to cube the brisket into bite-sized pieces, about 1-2 inches in size.
   Place the cubed brisket (burnt ends) in a large disposable aluminum pan or a cast iron skillet. Pour your favorite barbecue sauce over the burnt ends, tossing to coat evenly.
   Return the pan or skillet to the smoker and cook the burnt ends for an additional 1-2 hours, or until they are caramelized and tender. Stir occasionally to prevent burning and ensure even coating with the sauce.

Once the burnt ends are caramelized and tender, remove them from the smoker and transfer them to a serving platter.
Serve the Kansas City-style burnt ends hot, as a delicious appetizer, side dish, or main course. Enjoy the smoky, sweet, and savory flavor of these barbecue delights!

These Kansas City-style burnt ends are sure to be a hit at your next barbecue or gathering. Enjoy the rich, smoky flavor and tender texture of this barbecue classic!

Bourbon-Marinated Grilled Steak

Ingredients:

- 4 steaks of your choice (such as ribeye, New York strip, or filet mignon)
- 1/2 cup bourbon whiskey
- 1/4 cup soy sauce
- 1/4 cup olive oil
- 2 tablespoons Worcestershire sauce
- 2 cloves garlic, minced
- 1 tablespoon brown sugar
- 1 teaspoon black pepper
- 1 teaspoon dried thyme
- Salt, to taste

Instructions:

1. Prepare the Marinade:

    In a bowl, whisk together the bourbon whiskey, soy sauce, olive oil, Worcestershire sauce, minced garlic, brown sugar, black pepper, and dried thyme until well combined.

    Place the steaks in a shallow dish or a large resealable plastic bag.

    Pour the marinade over the steaks, making sure they are fully coated. Cover the dish or seal the bag and refrigerate for at least 2 hours, or preferably overnight, to allow the flavors to penetrate the meat.

2. Preheat the Grill:

    Preheat your grill to high heat, around 400-450°F (200-230°C).

3. Grill the Steaks:

    Remove the steaks from the marinade and discard the excess marinade.

    Season the steaks with salt on both sides, to taste.

    Place the steaks on the preheated grill and cook for about 4-6 minutes per side, depending on the thickness of the steaks and your desired level of doneness. Use a meat thermometer to check for doneness – 130°F (54°C) for medium-rare, 140°F (60°C) for medium, and 150°F (66°C) for medium-well.

    For perfect grill marks, rotate the steaks 45 degrees halfway through grilling on each side.

Once the steaks are cooked to your liking, remove them from the grill and let them rest for a few minutes before serving. This allows the juices to redistribute throughout the meat, ensuring a juicy and flavorful steak.

4. Serve:

Slice the grilled steaks against the grain into thin strips.
Serve the bourbon-marinated grilled steak hot, with your favorite side dishes such as grilled vegetables, mashed potatoes, or a fresh salad.
Optionally, you can drizzle any remaining marinade over the sliced steaks for added flavor.
Enjoy your delicious bourbon-marinated grilled steak with its rich and savory flavor, perfect for a special occasion or any time you want to treat yourself to a gourmet meal!

Southern BBQ Chicken Drumsticks

Ingredients:

- 8 chicken drumsticks
- Salt and black pepper, to taste
- 1 cup barbecue sauce (your favorite store-bought or homemade)
- 2 tablespoons olive oil
- 2 cloves garlic, minced
- 1 tablespoon paprika
- 1 tablespoon brown sugar
- 1 teaspoon onion powder
- 1 teaspoon garlic powder
- 1/2 teaspoon cayenne pepper (optional, for heat)
- Chopped fresh parsley or cilantro, for garnish (optional)

Instructions:

1. Marinate the Chicken Drumsticks:

    In a large bowl, combine the olive oil, minced garlic, paprika, brown sugar, onion powder, garlic powder, salt, black pepper, and cayenne pepper (if using). Mix well to make a marinade.
    Add the chicken drumsticks to the bowl with the marinade, tossing to coat the drumsticks evenly. Cover the bowl and refrigerate for at least 1 hour, or overnight for maximum flavor.

2. Preheat the Grill:

    Preheat your grill to medium-high heat, around 375-400°F (190-200°C). If using charcoal, wait until the coals are covered with white ash before cooking.

3. Grill the Chicken Drumsticks:

    Remove the marinated chicken drumsticks from the refrigerator and let them sit at room temperature for about 10-15 minutes while the grill preheats.
    Once the grill is hot, grease the grill grates with oil to prevent sticking.
    Place the chicken drumsticks on the grill, directly over the heat. Close the lid and cook for about 8-10 minutes on each side, or until the chicken is cooked through and reaches an internal temperature of 165°F (74°C).

During the last few minutes of grilling, brush the chicken drumsticks with barbecue sauce, turning them occasionally to ensure even coating. Reserve some sauce for serving.

4. Serve:

   Once the chicken drumsticks are fully cooked and glazed with barbecue sauce, remove them from the grill and transfer to a serving platter.
   Garnish the chicken drumsticks with chopped fresh parsley or cilantro, if desired.
   Serve hot, with extra barbecue sauce on the side for dipping.
   Enjoy your delicious Southern BBQ chicken drumsticks with their irresistible combination of smoky, sweet, and tangy flavors! They're perfect for a backyard barbecue, picnic, or any occasion when you want to enjoy tasty grilled chicken.

Smoked Sausage with Sweet and Spicy BBQ Sauce

Ingredients:

- 1 pound smoked sausage (such as kielbasa or andouille), sliced into rounds
- 1 cup barbecue sauce (your favorite store-bought or homemade)
- 2 tablespoons honey
- 1 tablespoon brown sugar
- 1 tablespoon Dijon mustard
- 1 teaspoon hot sauce (adjust to taste)
- 1/2 teaspoon smoked paprika
- Salt and black pepper, to taste
- Wooden skewers (optional, for grilling)

Instructions:

1. Prepare the Sweet and Spicy BBQ Sauce:

    In a small saucepan, combine the barbecue sauce, honey, brown sugar, Dijon mustard, hot sauce, and smoked paprika. Stir well to combine.
    Place the saucepan over medium heat and bring the mixture to a simmer. Let it cook for 5-7 minutes, stirring occasionally, until the sauce has thickened slightly and the flavors have melded together.
    Taste the sauce and adjust the seasoning, adding salt, black pepper, or more hot sauce as needed to suit your preferences. Remove the saucepan from the heat and set aside.

2. Prepare the Smoked Sausage:

    If you're grilling, preheat your grill to medium-high heat. If you're smoking, prepare your smoker according to manufacturer's instructions and preheat it to 250-275°F (120-135°C).
    Thread the sliced smoked sausage rounds onto wooden skewers if you're grilling, or you can simply place them directly on the grill grates or smoker racks.
    If grilling, brush the sausage rounds lightly with olive oil to prevent sticking. If smoking, you can skip this step.

3. Grill or Smoke the Sausage:

    Place the skewered or directly placed smoked sausage on the preheated grill or smoker.

If grilling, cook the sausage rounds for 3-4 minutes on each side, or until they are nicely browned and heated through. If smoking, cook the sausage for about 30-45 minutes, or until they are heated through and have absorbed some of the smoky flavor.

During the last few minutes of cooking, brush the smoked sausage rounds generously with the sweet and spicy BBQ sauce, turning them occasionally to ensure even coating.

4. Serve:

Once the smoked sausage rounds are cooked through and glazed with the BBQ sauce, remove them from the grill or smoker and transfer them to a serving platter.

Serve hot, with extra BBQ sauce on the side for dipping.

Enjoy your delicious smoked sausage with sweet and spicy BBQ sauce! It's perfect as a main dish, appetizer, or addition to a barbecue feast.

BBQ Pulled Chicken Sliders with Coleslaw

Ingredients:

For the BBQ Pulled Chicken:

- 2 lbs boneless, skinless chicken breasts or thighs
- 1 cup barbecue sauce (your favorite store-bought or homemade)
- 1/2 cup chicken broth or water
- 2 cloves garlic, minced
- 1 tablespoon brown sugar
- 1 tablespoon apple cider vinegar
- 1 teaspoon smoked paprika
- 1/2 teaspoon onion powder
- 1/2 teaspoon garlic powder
- Salt and pepper to taste

For the Coleslaw:

- 3 cups shredded cabbage (green or a mix of green and purple cabbage)
- 1 cup shredded carrots
- 1/2 cup mayonnaise
- 2 tablespoons apple cider vinegar
- 1 tablespoon honey
- Salt and pepper to taste

For the Sliders:

- Slider buns or small dinner rolls
- Butter, for toasting the buns (optional)
- Sliced pickles (optional, for serving)

Instructions:

1. Prepare the BBQ Pulled Chicken:

    In a slow cooker or crockpot, combine the barbecue sauce, chicken broth or water, minced garlic, brown sugar, apple cider vinegar, smoked paprika, onion powder, garlic powder, salt, and pepper. Mix well to combine.
    Add the chicken breasts or thighs to the slow cooker and coat them with the BBQ sauce mixture.

Cover and cook on low for 6-8 hours or on high for 3-4 hours, or until the chicken is tender and easily shreds with a fork.

Once the chicken is cooked, use two forks to shred it directly in the slow cooker, mixing it with the BBQ sauce.

2. Prepare the Coleslaw:

In a large mixing bowl, combine the shredded cabbage and carrots.

In a separate small bowl, whisk together the mayonnaise, apple cider vinegar, honey, salt, and pepper until well combined.

Pour the dressing over the cabbage and carrots, tossing until everything is evenly coated.

Cover and refrigerate the coleslaw until ready to use.

3. Assemble the Sliders:

If desired, lightly toast the slider buns or dinner rolls in a skillet with a little butter until golden brown.

Place a generous portion of BBQ pulled chicken on the bottom half of each slider bun.

Top the chicken with a scoop of coleslaw.

If desired, add a few slices of pickles on top of the coleslaw.

Place the top half of the slider bun on top to complete the sliders.

Serve the BBQ pulled chicken sliders with coleslaw immediately and enjoy!

These sliders are perfect for parties, potlucks, or weeknight dinners. They're packed with flavor and sure to be a hit with everyone!

Grilled Corn on the Cob with Chili Lime Butter

Ingredients:

- 4 ears of corn, husks removed
- 4 tablespoons unsalted butter, softened
- 1 tablespoon fresh lime juice
- 1 teaspoon lime zest
- 1 teaspoon chili powder
- 1/2 teaspoon paprika
- 1/4 teaspoon cayenne pepper (optional, for extra heat)
- Salt to taste
- Fresh cilantro or parsley, chopped (for garnish)

Instructions:

1. Prepare the Chili Lime Butter:

    In a small bowl, combine the softened butter, fresh lime juice, lime zest, chili powder, paprika, cayenne pepper (if using), and salt to taste. Mix until well combined.
    Taste the chili lime butter and adjust the seasoning as needed, adding more salt or lime juice if desired. Set aside.

2. Grill the Corn:

    Preheat your grill to medium-high heat.
    Place the husked ears of corn directly on the grill grates. Grill the corn for about 10-12 minutes, turning occasionally, until the kernels are tender and charred in spots.
    Remove the grilled corn from the grill and transfer them to a serving platter.

3. Finish with Chili Lime Butter:

    While the corn is still hot, generously spread the chili lime butter over each ear of corn, using a spoon or a brush to ensure even coating.
    Sprinkle chopped fresh cilantro or parsley over the buttered corn for garnish.
    Serve the grilled corn on the cob with chili lime butter immediately while hot.
    Enjoy your flavorful and delicious grilled corn on the cob with chili lime butter as a tasty side dish for your summer barbecue or cookout!

This dish adds a zesty and spicy twist to classic grilled corn, making it a favorite among guests and family members alike.

Southern-Style BBQ Baked Beans

Ingredients:

- 4 slices bacon, diced
- 1 small onion, diced
- 1/2 green bell pepper, diced
- 1/2 red bell pepper, diced
- 2 cans (15 ounces each) navy beans or pinto beans, drained and rinsed
- 1/2 cup barbecue sauce (your favorite store-bought or homemade)
- 1/4 cup ketchup
- 2 tablespoons brown sugar
- 1 tablespoon Worcestershire sauce
- 1 tablespoon apple cider vinegar
- 1 teaspoon Dijon mustard
- Salt and black pepper, to taste
- Optional toppings: sliced green onions, chopped fresh parsley, or crispy fried onions

Instructions:

Preheat your oven to 350°F (175°C). Lightly grease a baking dish or casserole dish with cooking spray or butter.

In a large skillet, cook the diced bacon over medium heat until crispy. Remove the cooked bacon from the skillet and set it aside on a paper towel-lined plate to drain excess grease.

In the same skillet with the bacon drippings, add the diced onion, green bell pepper, and red bell pepper. Cook for 3-4 minutes, or until the vegetables are softened.

In a large mixing bowl, combine the cooked bacon, sautéed vegetables, drained beans, barbecue sauce, ketchup, brown sugar, Worcestershire sauce, apple cider vinegar, Dijon mustard, salt, and black pepper. Stir until all ingredients are well combined.

Transfer the bean mixture to the prepared baking dish, spreading it out evenly.

Cover the baking dish with aluminum foil and bake in the preheated oven for 45 minutes.

After 45 minutes, remove the foil and continue baking for an additional 15-20 minutes, or until the beans are bubbly and the sauce has thickened.

Remove the baked beans from the oven and let them cool slightly before serving.

Garnish the baked beans with optional toppings such as sliced green onions, chopped fresh parsley, or crispy fried onions before serving, if desired.
Serve the Southern-style BBQ baked beans hot as a delicious side dish to accompany grilled meats, sandwiches, or other barbecue favorites.

These BBQ baked beans are rich, flavorful, and sure to be a hit at your next gathering! Enjoy the comforting taste of Southern-style comfort food with this classic dish.

BBQ Pork Belly Burnt Ends

Ingredients:

- 2 lbs pork belly, preferably skin removed
- BBQ rub of your choice
- BBQ sauce of your choice
- Wood chips for smoking (applewood or hickory work well)

Instructions:

Prepare the Pork Belly:
- Preheat your smoker to 250°F (120°C).
- While the smoker is heating up, cut the pork belly into 1-inch cubes.
- Season the cubes generously with your favorite BBQ rub. Make sure to coat each piece evenly.

Smoke the Pork Belly:
- Place the seasoned pork belly cubes on the smoker racks, making sure they are spread out evenly to allow for good airflow.
- Add your preferred wood chips to the smoker for that authentic smoky flavor.
- Close the smoker and let the pork belly smoke for about 2-3 hours. Check periodically and rotate the pieces if needed for even cooking.

Wrap and Continue Cooking:
- After the initial smoking period, remove the pork belly cubes from the smoker.
- Wrap them tightly in aluminum foil to help them retain moisture.
- Place the wrapped pork belly back on the smoker and continue cooking for another 1-2 hours, or until they are tender and have developed a nice bark.

Glaze and Finish:
- Carefully remove the foil-wrapped pork belly from the smoker.
- Unwrap the cubes and place them in a mixing bowl.
- Pour your favorite BBQ sauce over the cubes and toss them gently to coat evenly.
- Return the glazed pork belly cubes to the smoker for an additional 30 minutes to allow the sauce to caramelize and create a sticky glaze.

Serve:
- Once the BBQ pork belly burnt ends are done, remove them from the smoker and let them rest for a few minutes.

- Serve hot as a delicious appetizer or main dish, garnished with chopped fresh parsley or green onions if desired.

Enjoy your mouthwatering BBQ Pork Belly Burnt Ends! They're perfect for any barbecue gathering or game day feast.

Carolina Mustard BBQ Sauce

Ingredients:

- 1 cup yellow mustard
- 1/2 cup apple cider vinegar
- 1/4 cup honey
- 1/4 cup brown sugar
- 2 tablespoons Worcestershire sauce
- 1 tablespoon hot sauce (adjust to taste)
- 1 teaspoon garlic powder
- 1 teaspoon onion powder
- 1 teaspoon smoked paprika
- Salt and black pepper to taste

Instructions:

Combine Ingredients:
- In a medium saucepan, whisk together the yellow mustard, apple cider vinegar, honey, brown sugar, Worcestershire sauce, hot sauce, garlic powder, onion powder, and smoked paprika until well combined.

Simmer:
- Place the saucepan over medium heat and bring the mixture to a gentle simmer, stirring occasionally.

Cook and Thicken:
- Allow the sauce to simmer for about 10-15 minutes, or until it has thickened to your desired consistency. Keep in mind that the sauce will thicken further as it cools.

Season:
- Taste the sauce and season with salt and black pepper according to your preference. Adjust the sweetness or spiciness by adding more honey or hot sauce if desired.

Cool and Store:
- Once the sauce has reached your desired consistency and flavor, remove it from the heat and let it cool completely.
- Transfer the Carolina Mustard BBQ Sauce to a clean, airtight container or jar and store it in the refrigerator until ready to use. It can be stored for up to a few weeks.

Serve:
- Use the Carolina Mustard BBQ Sauce as a delicious dipping sauce for BBQ meats such as pulled pork, ribs, or chicken. It also works well as a marinade or basting sauce for grilling or smoking meats.

Enjoy your homemade Carolina Mustard BBQ Sauce, and add a touch of Southern flair to your barbecue dishes!

Classic Southern Potato Salad

Ingredients:

- 2 pounds (about 4 medium) russet potatoes, peeled and diced into 1-inch cubes
- 3 large eggs
- 1 cup mayonnaise
- 2 tablespoons yellow mustard
- 2 tablespoons sweet pickle relish
- 1/2 cup finely chopped celery
- 1/2 cup finely chopped red onion
- 1/4 cup chopped fresh parsley
- 1 tablespoon apple cider vinegar
- 1 teaspoon sugar
- Salt and black pepper to taste
- Paprika (for garnish, optional)

Instructions:

Boil Potatoes and Eggs:
- Place the diced potatoes in a large pot and cover them with water. Add a pinch of salt to the water.
- Bring the water to a boil over medium-high heat, then reduce the heat to medium-low and let the potatoes simmer for about 10-12 minutes, or until they are fork-tender but not mushy.
- In a separate pot, place the eggs and cover them with water. Bring the water to a boil, then remove the pot from the heat, cover it, and let the eggs sit in the hot water for about 10-12 minutes.
- Once the eggs are done, drain the water and let them cool before peeling and chopping them.

Prepare Dressing:
- In a small bowl, mix together the mayonnaise, yellow mustard, sweet pickle relish, apple cider vinegar, sugar, salt, and black pepper to create the dressing. Adjust the seasoning to taste.

Combine Ingredients:
- In a large mixing bowl, add the cooked and drained potatoes, chopped hard-boiled eggs, celery, red onion, and chopped parsley.
- Pour the prepared dressing over the potato mixture and gently toss until everything is evenly coated with the dressing.

Chill:

- Cover the bowl with plastic wrap or a lid and refrigerate the potato salad for at least 1-2 hours before serving. Chilling allows the flavors to meld together.

Serve:
- Before serving, give the potato salad a final stir and taste for seasoning. Adjust if necessary.
- Garnish with a sprinkle of paprika for color if desired.
- Serve chilled as a side dish at picnics, barbecues, or alongside your favorite Southern meals.

Enjoy your Classic Southern Potato Salad, a delicious and comforting addition to any meal!

Grilled Sweet Tea-Brined Chicken

Ingredients:

- 4 boneless, skinless chicken breasts
- 4 cups water
- 4 black tea bags
- 1/2 cup granulated sugar
- 1/4 cup kosher salt
- 1 lemon, sliced
- 2 cloves garlic, minced
- 1 teaspoon black peppercorns
- 1 teaspoon whole cloves
- 1 teaspoon dried thyme
- Olive oil (for brushing)
- Salt and black pepper (to taste)
- Lemon wedges (for serving, optional)
- Fresh parsley or thyme (for garnish, optional)

Instructions:

Prepare the Brine:
- In a large saucepan, bring the water to a boil. Once boiling, turn off the heat and add the black tea bags, sugar, kosher salt, sliced lemon, minced garlic, black peppercorns, whole cloves, and dried thyme.
- Stir to combine and let the mixture steep for about 5-10 minutes.

Cool the Brine:
- Remove the tea bags and discard them. Allow the brine to cool to room temperature.

Brine the Chicken:
- Place the chicken breasts in a large resealable plastic bag or a shallow dish.
- Pour the cooled sweet tea brine over the chicken, making sure it's completely submerged.
- Seal the bag or cover the dish with plastic wrap and refrigerate for at least 4 hours or overnight to allow the chicken to absorb the flavors.

Preheat the Grill:
- Preheat your grill to medium-high heat (about 375-400°F or 190-200°C).

Grill the Chicken:

- Remove the chicken from the brine and discard the brine. Pat the chicken dry with paper towels.
- Brush both sides of the chicken breasts lightly with olive oil and season with salt and black pepper to taste.
- Place the chicken breasts on the preheated grill and cook for 6-8 minutes per side, or until the internal temperature reaches 165°F (74°C) and the chicken is cooked through. Cooking time may vary depending on the thickness of the chicken breasts.
- Remove the chicken from the grill and let it rest for a few minutes before serving.

Serve:
- Serve the grilled sweet tea-brined chicken hot, garnished with fresh parsley or thyme if desired. Serve with lemon wedges on the side for an extra burst of flavor.

Enjoy your Grilled Sweet Tea-Brined Chicken, a delicious and unique twist on classic grilled chicken!

Texas BBQ Beef Ribs

Ingredients:

- 4-5 pounds beef back ribs or beef short ribs
- 2 tablespoons kosher salt
- 2 tablespoons freshly ground black pepper
- 2 tablespoons paprika
- 1 tablespoon garlic powder
- 1 tablespoon onion powder
- 1 tablespoon brown sugar
- 1 teaspoon cayenne pepper (optional, for heat)
- BBQ sauce (optional, for serving)

Instructions:

Prepare the Ribs:
- Remove the membrane from the back of the ribs, if present. This helps the rub penetrate the meat better and allows for better flavor absorption.
- Pat the ribs dry with paper towels.

Make the Rub:
- In a small bowl, mix together the kosher salt, black pepper, paprika, garlic powder, onion powder, brown sugar, and cayenne pepper (if using) to create the dry rub.

Season the Ribs:
- Generously coat the ribs on all sides with the dry rub, pressing the rub into the meat to ensure it adheres well.
- Let the ribs sit at room temperature for about 30 minutes to allow the flavors to penetrate the meat.

Prepare the Smoker:
- Preheat your smoker to 250°F (120°C). Use wood chips or chunks of your choice (such as oak, hickory, or mesquite) for smoking.

Smoke the Ribs:
- Place the seasoned ribs directly on the smoker grate, bone side down.
- Close the smoker and let the ribs smoke for about 4-5 hours, or until they are tender and the internal temperature reaches around 200°F (93°C).

Optional Wrap:
- If you prefer, you can wrap the ribs in aluminum foil after about 2-3 hours of smoking to help retain moisture and speed up the cooking process. This is known as the "Texas crutch."

Finish and Serve:
- Once the ribs are cooked to your liking and tender, remove them from the smoker.
- Let the ribs rest for about 10-15 minutes before slicing them into individual ribs.
- Serve the Texas BBQ beef ribs hot, optionally with your favorite BBQ sauce on the side for dipping.

Enjoy your delicious Texas-style BBQ beef ribs, a true barbecue favorite!

Smoked Mac and Cheese

Ingredients:

- 16 oz (about 450g) elbow macaroni or any pasta shape of your choice
- 1/4 cup (57g) unsalted butter
- 1/4 cup (30g) all-purpose flour
- 3 cups (720ml) whole milk
- 2 cups (240g) shredded sharp cheddar cheese
- 1 cup (120g) shredded Gruyere cheese (or substitute with more cheddar)
- 1/2 cup (60g) grated Parmesan cheese
- 1 teaspoon Dijon mustard
- 1/2 teaspoon garlic powder
- 1/2 teaspoon onion powder
- Salt and black pepper to taste
- Cooking spray or butter for greasing
- Optional toppings: bread crumbs, crispy bacon bits, chopped parsley

Instructions:

Preheat the Smoker:
- Preheat your smoker to 225°F (107°C) using your choice of wood chips or chunks. Hickory, applewood, or oak work well for smoked mac and cheese.

Cook the Pasta:
- Cook the pasta according to the package instructions in a large pot of salted boiling water until al dente. Drain the pasta and set it aside.

Prepare the Cheese Sauce:
- In a large saucepan, melt the butter over medium heat. Once melted, whisk in the flour to create a roux. Cook the roux for 1-2 minutes, stirring constantly.
- Gradually pour in the milk, whisking continuously to prevent lumps from forming.
- Cook the sauce until it thickens and coats the back of a spoon, about 5-7 minutes.
- Reduce the heat to low and stir in the shredded cheddar cheese, Gruyere cheese (or more cheddar), and grated Parmesan cheese until melted and smooth.
- Stir in the Dijon mustard, garlic powder, onion powder, salt, and black pepper to taste.

Combine Pasta and Cheese Sauce:
- Add the cooked pasta to the cheese sauce and stir until the pasta is evenly coated with the cheese sauce.

Smoke the Mac and Cheese:
- Grease a large disposable aluminum foil pan or a cast iron skillet with cooking spray or butter.
- Transfer the mac and cheese mixture to the prepared pan or skillet, spreading it out evenly.
- Place the pan or skillet on the preheated smoker grate.

Smoke for Flavor:
- Close the smoker and let the mac and cheese smoke for about 1-1.5 hours, or until it is heated through and has absorbed a nice smoky flavor. Stir the mac and cheese occasionally to ensure even smoking.

Serve:
- Once the mac and cheese is smoked to your liking, remove it from the smoker.
- If desired, sprinkle with bread crumbs, crispy bacon bits, or chopped parsley as toppings.
- Serve the smoked mac and cheese hot as a delicious side dish or main course.

Enjoy your flavorful smoked mac and cheese, a perfect comfort food with a smoky twist!

Grilled Peach and Bourbon BBQ Pork Chops

Ingredients:

- 4 pork chops, about 1-inch thick
- Salt and black pepper, to taste
- 2 ripe peaches, halved and pitted
- 1 tablespoon olive oil
- 1/4 cup bourbon
- 1/2 cup barbecue sauce (homemade or store-bought)
- 2 tablespoons honey
- 2 cloves garlic, minced
- 1 teaspoon Dijon mustard
- Chopped fresh parsley or green onions, for garnish (optional)

Instructions:

Prepare the Pork Chops:
- Season the pork chops generously with salt and black pepper on both sides.

Prepare the Grilled Peaches:
- Brush the halved and pitted peaches with olive oil to prevent sticking.
- Preheat your grill to medium-high heat.
- Grill the peaches cut-side down for about 3-4 minutes, or until they have grill marks and are slightly softened. Remove them from the grill and set aside.

Grill the Pork Chops:
- Place the seasoned pork chops on the preheated grill.
- Grill the pork chops for about 4-5 minutes on each side, or until they are cooked through and reach an internal temperature of 145°F (63°C). Cooking time may vary depending on the thickness of the pork chops.

Prepare the Bourbon BBQ Sauce:
- In a small saucepan, combine the bourbon, barbecue sauce, honey, minced garlic, and Dijon mustard.
- Place the saucepan over medium heat and simmer the sauce for about 5-7 minutes, stirring occasionally, until it thickens slightly and the alcohol cooks off. Remove from heat.

Glaze the Pork Chops:
- Brush the grilled peaches with the prepared bourbon BBQ sauce, reserving some sauce for serving.

- Continue grilling the pork chops for an additional 1-2 minutes on each side, brushing them with the bourbon BBQ sauce during the last few minutes of grilling to glaze them.

Serve:
- Remove the grilled pork chops and peaches from the grill.
- Serve the pork chops with the grilled peaches on the side.
- Drizzle the remaining bourbon BBQ sauce over the pork chops and peaches.
- Garnish with chopped fresh parsley or green onions if desired.
- Serve hot and enjoy your Grilled Peach and Bourbon BBQ Pork Chops!

This dish pairs wonderfully with your favorite sides, such as grilled vegetables, cornbread, or a fresh salad.

Spicy Cajun BBQ Shrimp Po' Boys

Ingredients:

For the Cajun BBQ Shrimp:

- 1 pound large shrimp, peeled and deveined
- 2 tablespoons Cajun seasoning
- 2 tablespoons olive oil
- 1/4 cup barbecue sauce
- 1 tablespoon Worcestershire sauce
- 2 cloves garlic, minced
- Salt and pepper to taste

For the Sandwiches:

- 4 to 6 Po' Boy rolls or French baguettes, split lengthwise
- 1/2 cup mayonnaise
- 2 tablespoons hot sauce (adjust to taste)
- Shredded lettuce
- Sliced tomatoes
- Sliced pickles
- Sliced red onion (optional)
- Lemon wedges for garnish (optional)
- Chopped parsley for garnish (optional)

Instructions:

Prepare the Cajun BBQ Shrimp:
- In a mixing bowl, combine the shrimp with Cajun seasoning, olive oil, barbecue sauce, Worcestershire sauce, minced garlic, salt, and pepper. Toss to coat the shrimp evenly. Let the shrimp marinate for about 15-20 minutes.

Cook the Shrimp:
- Heat a large skillet or grill pan over medium-high heat. Add the marinated shrimp to the skillet in a single layer.
- Cook the shrimp for 2-3 minutes on each side, or until they are pink and cooked through. Be careful not to overcook the shrimp, as they can become tough.

Prepare the Sandwiches:
- In a small bowl, mix together mayonnaise and hot sauce to create a spicy mayo spread. Adjust the amount of hot sauce to suit your taste preference.
- Spread the spicy mayo onto the split Po' Boy rolls or French baguettes.
- Place a layer of shredded lettuce on the bottom half of each roll, followed by sliced tomatoes, pickles, and sliced red onion if desired.
- Arrange the cooked Cajun BBQ shrimp on top of the vegetables.

Assemble the Po' Boys:
- Close the sandwiches with the top halves of the rolls.
- Serve the Spicy Cajun BBQ Shrimp Po' Boys immediately, garnished with lemon wedges and chopped parsley if desired.

Serve and Enjoy:
- Serve the sandwiches immediately while they're still warm and enjoy the bold flavors of Cajun seasoning and barbecue sauce with succulent shrimp, all nestled in a soft Po' Boy roll.

These Spicy Cajun BBQ Shrimp Po' Boys make a fantastic meal for lunch or dinner, especially when served with a side of coleslaw or sweet potato fries. Enjoy the delicious flavors of the South in every bite!

Smoked Pork Shoulder with Carolina Vinegar Sauce

Ingredients:

For the Smoked Pork Shoulder:

- 1 (6-8 pound) pork shoulder (also known as pork butt or Boston butt), bone-in or boneless
- 2 tablespoons paprika
- 2 tablespoons brown sugar
- 2 tablespoons kosher salt
- 1 tablespoon garlic powder
- 1 tablespoon onion powder
- 1 tablespoon black pepper
- 1 teaspoon cayenne pepper (optional, for heat)
- Wood chips or chunks for smoking (hickory, apple, or cherry wood)

For the Carolina Vinegar Sauce:

- 1 cup apple cider vinegar
- 1/4 cup ketchup
- 2 tablespoons brown sugar
- 1 tablespoon Worcestershire sauce
- 1 tablespoon hot sauce (such as Tabasco or Texas Pete)
- 1 teaspoon red pepper flakes
- 1 teaspoon salt
- 1 teaspoon black pepper
- 1 teaspoon garlic powder
- 1 teaspoon onion powder

Instructions:

Prepare the Pork Shoulder:
- In a small bowl, mix together the paprika, brown sugar, kosher salt, garlic powder, onion powder, black pepper, and cayenne pepper (if using) to create the dry rub.
- Pat the pork shoulder dry with paper towels, then rub the dry rub mixture all over the pork shoulder, coating it evenly. Allow the pork shoulder to

marinate in the rub for at least 1 hour, or overnight in the refrigerator for deeper flavor.

Preheat the Smoker:
- Preheat your smoker to 225°F (107°C). Use wood chips or chunks of your choice (such as hickory, apple, or cherry wood) for smoking.

Smoke the Pork Shoulder:
- Once the smoker is preheated, place the pork shoulder on the smoker rack, fat side up.
- Insert a meat thermometer into the thickest part of the pork shoulder, being careful not to touch the bone.
- Close the smoker and let the pork shoulder smoke for several hours, approximately 1.5 to 2 hours per pound, or until the internal temperature reaches at least 195°F (91°C) and the meat is tender enough to pull apart easily with a fork.

Prepare the Carolina Vinegar Sauce:
- In a medium saucepan, combine the apple cider vinegar, ketchup, brown sugar, Worcestershire sauce, hot sauce, red pepper flakes, salt, black pepper, garlic powder, and onion powder.
- Bring the mixture to a simmer over medium heat, stirring occasionally, and let it cook for about 5-7 minutes to allow the flavors to meld together. Remove from heat.

Serve:
- Once the pork shoulder is done smoking and reaches the desired internal temperature, remove it from the smoker and let it rest for about 20-30 minutes.
- After resting, use two forks to shred the smoked pork shoulder into bite-sized pieces.
- Serve the smoked pork shoulder with the Carolina vinegar sauce on the side or drizzled over the top. You can also serve it on sandwich buns with coleslaw for a classic Carolina-style pulled pork sandwich.

Enjoy your delicious Smoked Pork Shoulder with Carolina Vinegar Sauce, a perfect dish for any barbecue or gathering!

Alabama BBQ Chicken Sliders with White BBQ Sauce

Ingredients:

For the Chicken:

- 1 pound boneless, skinless chicken breasts or thighs
- Salt and pepper to taste
- 1 tablespoon olive oil
- 1 cup barbecue sauce (homemade or store-bought)

For the White BBQ Sauce:

- 1 cup mayonnaise
- 1/4 cup apple cider vinegar
- 2 tablespoons lemon juice
- 1 tablespoon Dijon mustard
- 1 tablespoon honey
- 1 teaspoon garlic powder
- 1 teaspoon onion powder
- Salt and pepper to taste

For the Sliders:

- Slider buns or dinner rolls
- Sliced pickles
- Sliced red onion (optional)
- Lettuce leaves (optional)

Instructions:

Prepare the Chicken:
- Season the chicken breasts or thighs with salt and pepper on both sides.
- Heat olive oil in a skillet or grill pan over medium-high heat.
- Cook the chicken for 4-5 minutes on each side, or until cooked through and no longer pink in the center.
- Once cooked, remove the chicken from the skillet and let it rest for a few minutes. Then, shred the chicken using two forks.

Make the White BBQ Sauce:

- In a mixing bowl, combine mayonnaise, apple cider vinegar, lemon juice, Dijon mustard, honey, garlic powder, onion powder, salt, and pepper. Mix well until smooth and creamy. Adjust seasoning to taste.

Assemble the Sliders:
- Split the slider buns or dinner rolls in half horizontally.
- Place a spoonful of shredded chicken on the bottom half of each bun.
- Drizzle a generous amount of white BBQ sauce over the chicken.
- Top with sliced pickles, sliced red onion (if using), and lettuce leaves (if desired).
- Cover with the top half of the bun.

Serve:
- Arrange the assembled sliders on a serving platter.
- Serve immediately, and enjoy your Alabama BBQ Chicken Sliders with White BBQ Sauce!

These sliders make a fantastic appetizer, party food, or main course for any occasion. The tangy and creamy white BBQ sauce adds a unique and delicious flavor to the juicy chicken. Pair them with your favorite side dishes, such as coleslaw or potato salad, for a complete meal.

BBQ Pulled Chicken Nachos

Ingredients:

- 1 pound boneless, skinless chicken breasts or thighs
- Salt and pepper to taste
- 1 cup barbecue sauce (homemade or store-bought)
- Tortilla chips
- 1 cup shredded cheese (cheddar, Monterey Jack, or a blend)
- 1/2 cup diced tomatoes
- 1/4 cup diced red onion
- 1/4 cup sliced jalapeños (optional)
- 1/4 cup chopped fresh cilantro (optional)
- Sour cream, guacamole, and salsa for serving (optional)

Instructions:

Prepare the BBQ Pulled Chicken:
- Season the chicken breasts or thighs with salt and pepper on both sides.
- Place the seasoned chicken in a slow cooker or Instant Pot.
- Pour the barbecue sauce over the chicken, making sure it's well coated.
- Cook the chicken in the slow cooker on low for 6-8 hours or on high for 3-4 hours until it's tender and easily shreddable. If using an Instant Pot, cook on high pressure for 15-20 minutes, then quick release the pressure.
- Once cooked, shred the chicken using two forks. Mix it with the barbecue sauce in the slow cooker or Instant Pot to coat evenly.

Assemble the Nachos:
- Preheat the oven to 375°F (190°C).
- Arrange the tortilla chips in a single layer on a large baking sheet or oven-safe dish.
- Sprinkle the shredded cheese evenly over the tortilla chips.
- Spoon the BBQ pulled chicken over the cheese-covered tortilla chips.

Add Toppings:
- Sprinkle diced tomatoes, diced red onion, and sliced jalapeños (if using) over the pulled chicken.
- For extra flavor, you can also sprinkle chopped fresh cilantro on top.

Bake:
- Place the baking sheet or dish in the preheated oven and bake for 10-12 minutes, or until the cheese is melted and bubbly.

Serve:

- Once the nachos are done baking, remove them from the oven.
- Serve the BBQ Pulled Chicken Nachos hot, with optional toppings such as sour cream, guacamole, and salsa on the side.

Enjoy these delicious BBQ Pulled Chicken Nachos as a tasty appetizer, snack, or even a meal on their own. They're sure to be a hit at any gathering!

Southern BBQ Spare Ribs

Ingredients:

For the ribs:

- 2 racks of spare ribs (about 4-5 pounds total)
- Salt and black pepper to taste
- 2 tablespoons brown sugar
- 2 tablespoons paprika
- 1 tablespoon garlic powder
- 1 tablespoon onion powder
- 1 teaspoon cayenne pepper (optional, for heat)

For the barbecue sauce:

- 1 cup ketchup
- 1/2 cup apple cider vinegar
- 1/4 cup brown sugar
- 2 tablespoons Worcestershire sauce
- 1 tablespoon Dijon mustard
- 1 tablespoon molasses
- 1 teaspoon smoked paprika
- 1 teaspoon garlic powder
- Salt and black pepper to taste

Instructions:

Prepare the Ribs:
- Preheat your grill or smoker to 250°F (120°C).
- Remove the membrane from the back of the ribs if it's still attached. This helps the rub penetrate the meat better.
- Season the ribs generously with salt and black pepper on both sides.

Make the Dry Rub:
- In a small bowl, mix together the brown sugar, paprika, garlic powder, onion powder, and cayenne pepper (if using) to create the dry rub.
- Rub the mixture evenly over both sides of the ribs.

Smoke the Ribs:
- Place the seasoned ribs on the grill or smoker, bone side down.

- Close the lid and let the ribs smoke for about 3-4 hours, or until they are tender and the meat has pulled back from the bones.

Make the Barbecue Sauce:
- In a medium saucepan, combine the ketchup, apple cider vinegar, brown sugar, Worcestershire sauce, Dijon mustard, molasses, smoked paprika, garlic powder, salt, and black pepper.
- Bring the mixture to a simmer over medium heat, stirring occasionally. Let it cook for about 10-15 minutes, or until the sauce thickens slightly.

Glaze the Ribs:
- During the last 30 minutes of cooking, brush the ribs generously with the barbecue sauce on both sides.
- Continue cooking until the sauce caramelizes and forms a sticky glaze on the ribs.

Serve:
- Once the ribs are done, remove them from the grill or smoker and let them rest for a few minutes.
- Cut the ribs into individual portions and serve hot, with extra barbecue sauce on the side for dipping.

Enjoy your delicious Southern BBQ Spare Ribs, a true barbecue classic that's perfect for any occasion!

Grilled Watermelon Salad with Feta and Mint

Ingredients:

- 1 small seedless watermelon, sliced into wedges or cubes
- Olive oil, for brushing
- Salt and black pepper to taste
- 1/2 cup crumbled feta cheese
- Fresh mint leaves, torn or chopped
- Balsamic glaze, for drizzling (optional)

Instructions:

Prepare the Watermelon:
- Preheat your grill to medium-high heat.
- Brush the watermelon wedges or cubes lightly with olive oil on both sides.
- Season them with a sprinkle of salt and black pepper.

Grill the Watermelon:
- Place the watermelon slices on the preheated grill.
- Grill for about 2-3 minutes on each side, or until grill marks appear and the watermelon softens slightly. Be careful not to overcook; you want the watermelon to still hold its shape.

Assemble the Salad:
- Arrange the grilled watermelon on a serving platter or individual plates.
- Sprinkle crumbled feta cheese over the grilled watermelon.

Add Fresh Mint:
- Scatter torn or chopped fresh mint leaves over the salad. The mint adds a refreshing flavor that pairs beautifully with the sweetness of the watermelon and the saltiness of the feta cheese.

Drizzle with Balsamic Glaze (Optional):
- For an extra layer of flavor, drizzle balsamic glaze over the salad. The tangy sweetness of the balsamic glaze complements the other flavors in the salad beautifully.

Serve:
- Serve the Grilled Watermelon Salad with Feta and Mint immediately as a refreshing appetizer or side dish.

Enjoy the delightful combination of flavors and textures in this Grilled Watermelon Salad with Feta and Mint. It's a perfect dish for summer gatherings or as a light and refreshing addition to any meal!

Smoked Cornbread with Honey Butter

Ingredients:

For the smoked cornbread:

- 1 cup cornmeal
- 1 cup all-purpose flour
- 1 tablespoon baking powder
- 1/2 teaspoon baking soda
- 1/2 teaspoon salt
- 2 eggs
- 1 cup buttermilk
- 1/4 cup melted butter
- 1/4 cup honey

For the honey butter:

- 1/2 cup unsalted butter, softened
- 2 tablespoons honey
- Pinch of salt (optional)

Instructions:

Prepare the Smoker:
- Preheat your smoker to 350°F (175°C) using indirect heat. Add wood chips or chunks for smoking, such as hickory or applewood.

Prepare the Cornbread Batter:
- In a large mixing bowl, whisk together the cornmeal, flour, baking powder, baking soda, and salt.
- In a separate bowl, beat the eggs, then stir in the buttermilk, melted butter, and honey.
- Pour the wet ingredients into the dry ingredients and stir until just combined. Do not overmix; a few lumps are okay.

Smoke the Cornbread:
- Pour the cornbread batter into a greased cast iron skillet or baking dish.
- Place the skillet or dish in the preheated smoker.

- Close the smoker and bake the cornbread for about 25-30 minutes, or until a toothpick inserted into the center comes out clean and the top is golden brown.

Make the Honey Butter:
- While the cornbread is smoking, prepare the honey butter. In a small bowl, mix together the softened butter and honey until well combined. Taste and add a pinch of salt if desired.

Serve:
- Once the cornbread is done, remove it from the smoker and let it cool for a few minutes.
- Slice the smoked cornbread into wedges or squares and serve warm with the honey butter on the side.

Enjoy the delicious smoky flavor of the cornbread paired with the sweetness of the honey butter. It's perfect as a side dish for barbecue or any Southern meal, or as a tasty snack on its own!

BBQ Bacon-Wrapped Jalapeno Poppers

Ingredients:

- 12 jalapeño peppers
- 6 slices of bacon, cut in half crosswise
- 8 oz cream cheese, softened
- 1/2 cup shredded cheddar cheese
- 1/2 teaspoon garlic powder
- 1/2 teaspoon onion powder
- 1/4 teaspoon smoked paprika
- 1/4 teaspoon black pepper
- 1/4 cup barbecue sauce
- Toothpicks

Instructions:

Prepare the Jalapeños:
- Preheat your oven to 375°F (190°C). Line a baking sheet with parchment paper.
- Cut the jalapeños in half lengthwise and remove the seeds and membranes using a spoon. Wear gloves or wash your hands thoroughly after handling the jalapeños to avoid irritation.

Prepare the Filling:
- In a mixing bowl, combine the softened cream cheese, shredded cheddar cheese, garlic powder, onion powder, smoked paprika, and black pepper. Mix until well combined.

Fill the Jalapeños:
- Fill each jalapeño half with the cream cheese mixture, dividing it evenly among them.

Wrap with Bacon:
- Wrap each cream cheese-filled jalapeño half with a half slice of bacon, securing it with a toothpick.

Bake the Poppers:
- Place the bacon-wrapped jalapeño poppers on the prepared baking sheet.
- Bake in the preheated oven for 20-25 minutes, or until the bacon is crispy and the jalapeños are tender.

Glaze with Barbecue Sauce:
- Remove the jalapeño poppers from the oven and brush them with barbecue sauce.

- Return them to the oven and bake for an additional 5 minutes to allow the barbecue sauce to caramelize.

Serve:
- Remove the jalapeño poppers from the oven and let them cool for a few minutes before serving.
- Serve the BBQ Bacon-Wrapped Jalapeño Poppers warm as a tasty appetizer or snack.

Enjoy the spicy, cheesy, and smoky flavors of these BBQ Bacon-Wrapped Jalapeño Poppers at your next gathering or game day party!

Memphis-Style BBQ Pulled Pork Sandwiches

Ingredients:

For the Pulled Pork:

- 4-5 pounds pork shoulder (also known as pork butt), boneless or bone-in
- 2 tablespoons paprika
- 2 tablespoons brown sugar
- 1 tablespoon garlic powder
- 1 tablespoon onion powder
- 1 tablespoon chili powder
- 1 tablespoon cumin
- 1 tablespoon black pepper
- 1 tablespoon salt
- 1 cup apple cider vinegar
- 1 cup chicken or pork broth
- 1 cup barbecue sauce (Memphis-style or your favorite)

For the Sandwiches:

- Hamburger buns or sandwich rolls
- Coleslaw (optional, for topping)

Instructions:

Prepare the Pork Shoulder:
- In a small bowl, mix together the paprika, brown sugar, garlic powder, onion powder, chili powder, cumin, black pepper, and salt to create a dry rub.
- Rub the dry rub mixture all over the pork shoulder, coating it evenly. Allow the pork shoulder to marinate in the rub for at least 1 hour, or overnight in the refrigerator for deeper flavor.

Smoke or Slow Cook the Pork:
- Preheat your smoker to 225°F (107°C). Use wood chips or chunks for smoking, such as hickory or applewood.
- Place the pork shoulder on the smoker grate, fat side up, and smoke for about 6-8 hours, or until the internal temperature reaches 195-205°F (90-96°C) and the meat is tender enough to shred easily with a fork.

Alternatively, you can cook the pork in a slow cooker on low for 8-10 hours until tender.

Shred the Pork:
- Once the pork shoulder is cooked and tender, remove it from the smoker or slow cooker and let it rest for about 20-30 minutes.
- Use two forks to shred the pork shoulder into bite-sized pieces, discarding any large pieces of fat.

Prepare the Sauce:
- In a small saucepan, combine the apple cider vinegar, chicken or pork broth, and barbecue sauce. Heat the sauce over medium heat until warmed through.

Combine and Serve:
- Place the shredded pork in a large mixing bowl and pour the warm sauce over it. Toss until the pork is evenly coated with the sauce.
- Toast the hamburger buns or sandwich rolls, if desired.
- Assemble the sandwiches by placing a generous portion of the BBQ pulled pork on the bottom half of each bun.
- Top with coleslaw if desired, and cover with the top half of the bun.

Serve and Enjoy:
- Serve the Memphis-style BBQ pulled pork sandwiches immediately, and enjoy the delicious flavors of tender pulled pork and tangy barbecue sauce.

These Memphis-style BBQ pulled pork sandwiches are perfect for any occasion, whether it's a backyard barbecue, game day gathering, or weeknight dinner. Enjoy!

Texas BBQ Chili

Ingredients:

- 2 pounds beef chuck roast, cut into 1/2-inch cubes
- Salt and black pepper to taste
- 2 tablespoons vegetable oil
- 1 large onion, chopped
- 3 cloves garlic, minced
- 1 jalapeño pepper, seeded and diced
- 1 bell pepper, diced
- 2 tablespoons chili powder
- 1 tablespoon smoked paprika
- 1 teaspoon ground cumin
- 1 teaspoon dried oregano
- 1/2 teaspoon cayenne pepper (adjust to taste)
- 1 (15-ounce) can diced tomatoes
- 1 (15-ounce) can tomato sauce
- 1 (15-ounce) can kidney beans, drained and rinsed
- 1 (15-ounce) can black beans, drained and rinsed
- 1 cup beef broth
- 1/2 cup barbecue sauce (Texas-style or your favorite)
- Chopped fresh cilantro, for garnish (optional)
- Shredded cheddar cheese, for garnish (optional)
- Sliced jalapeños, for garnish (optional)
- Sour cream, for serving (optional)

Instructions:

Season and Brown the Beef:
- Season the beef cubes with salt and black pepper to taste.
- Heat the vegetable oil in a large pot or Dutch oven over medium-high heat.
- Add the seasoned beef cubes in batches and cook until browned on all sides. Remove the browned beef from the pot and set aside.

Sauté the Aromatics:
- In the same pot, add the chopped onion, minced garlic, diced jalapeño pepper, and diced bell pepper. Sauté until the vegetables are softened, about 5 minutes.

Add Spices and Tomatoes:

- Stir in the chili powder, smoked paprika, ground cumin, dried oregano, and cayenne pepper. Cook for an additional 1-2 minutes, until fragrant.
- Add the diced tomatoes (with their juices) and tomato sauce to the pot. Stir to combine, scraping up any browned bits from the bottom of the pot.

Simmer the Chili:
- Return the browned beef cubes to the pot.
- Add the drained and rinsed kidney beans and black beans.
- Pour in the beef broth and barbecue sauce, stirring to combine.
- Bring the chili to a simmer, then reduce the heat to low. Cover and let it simmer gently for about 1.5 to 2 hours, stirring occasionally, until the beef is tender and the flavors have melded together.

Serve:
- Ladle the Texas BBQ chili into bowls.
- Garnish with chopped fresh cilantro, shredded cheddar cheese, sliced jalapeños, and a dollop of sour cream, if desired.
- Serve hot and enjoy this delicious and comforting Texas-style BBQ chili!

This Texas BBQ chili is perfect for cozy evenings or gatherings with friends and family. It's full of bold flavors and guaranteed to satisfy your cravings for a hearty and comforting meal.

Bourbon BBQ Glazed Salmon

Ingredients:

For the Bourbon BBQ Glaze:

- 1/4 cup bourbon whiskey
- 1/4 cup barbecue sauce
- 2 tablespoons brown sugar
- 2 tablespoons soy sauce
- 1 tablespoon Dijon mustard
- 1 tablespoon Worcestershire sauce
- 2 cloves garlic, minced
- Salt and pepper to taste

For the Salmon:

- 4 salmon fillets, about 6 ounces each
- Salt and pepper to taste
- Olive oil, for brushing
- Fresh chopped parsley or green onions for garnish (optional)

Instructions:

Prepare the Bourbon BBQ Glaze:
- In a small saucepan, combine the bourbon whiskey, barbecue sauce, brown sugar, soy sauce, Dijon mustard, Worcestershire sauce, minced garlic, salt, and pepper.
- Stir well to combine.
- Place the saucepan over medium heat and bring the mixture to a simmer.
- Let it simmer for about 5-7 minutes, stirring occasionally, until the sauce has thickened slightly. Remove from heat and set aside.

Prepare the Salmon:
- Preheat your grill to medium-high heat.
- Season the salmon fillets with salt and pepper on both sides.
- Brush the salmon fillets lightly with olive oil to prevent sticking to the grill.

Grill the Salmon:
- Place the salmon fillets on the preheated grill, skin-side down if they have skin.

- Grill for about 4-5 minutes on each side, or until the salmon is cooked through and flakes easily with a fork. Cooking time may vary depending on the thickness of the fillets.

Glaze the Salmon:
- During the last few minutes of grilling, brush the bourbon BBQ glaze generously over the salmon fillets, reserving some glaze for serving.
- Continue cooking for another minute or two, allowing the glaze to caramelize slightly on the salmon.

Serve:
- Once the salmon is done, remove it from the grill.
- Transfer the glazed salmon fillets to a serving platter or individual plates.
- Drizzle any remaining bourbon BBQ glaze over the salmon.
- Garnish with fresh chopped parsley or green onions, if desired.

Enjoy:
- Serve the Bourbon BBQ Glazed Salmon hot, alongside your favorite side dishes, such as roasted vegetables, rice, or a salad.
- Enjoy the delicious combination of tender grilled salmon with the sweet and tangy bourbon BBQ glaze!

This Bourbon BBQ Glazed Salmon makes for an impressive and flavorful main course that's perfect for any occasion, from weeknight dinners to special gatherings.

Southern Coleslaw with Tangy Dressing

Ingredients:

For the Coleslaw:

- 1 small head of green cabbage, finely shredded (about 4 cups)
- 1 large carrot, grated
- 1/2 cup chopped green onions (optional)

For the Tangy Dressing:

- 1/2 cup mayonnaise
- 2 tablespoons apple cider vinegar
- 1 tablespoon Dijon mustard
- 1 tablespoon honey or granulated sugar
- 1/2 teaspoon celery seed
- Salt and black pepper to taste

Instructions:

Prepare the Coleslaw:
- In a large mixing bowl, combine the finely shredded cabbage, grated carrot, and chopped green onions (if using). Toss to mix well and set aside.

Make the Tangy Dressing:
- In a small bowl, whisk together the mayonnaise, apple cider vinegar, Dijon mustard, honey or sugar, and celery seed until smooth and well combined.
- Season with salt and black pepper to taste. Adjust the sweetness and tanginess according to your preference by adding more honey or apple cider vinegar if desired.

Combine Dressing with Coleslaw:
- Pour the tangy dressing over the cabbage mixture.
- Toss the coleslaw gently until the vegetables are evenly coated with the dressing.

Chill and Serve:
- Cover the bowl with plastic wrap or transfer the coleslaw to an airtight container.

- Refrigerate the coleslaw for at least 1 hour before serving to allow the flavors to meld together and the cabbage to soften slightly.

Serve:
- Once chilled, give the coleslaw a final toss.
- Serve the Southern coleslaw as a side dish alongside your favorite Southern main dishes, such as barbecue ribs, fried chicken, or pulled pork sandwiches.

Enjoy:
- Enjoy the tangy and crunchy goodness of this classic Southern coleslaw with tangy dressing!

This Southern coleslaw recipe is simple to make and bursting with flavor. It's the perfect accompaniment to any Southern meal or barbecue, and it's sure to be a hit with family and friends alike.

Grilled Okra with Cajun Seasoning

Ingredients:

- 1 pound fresh okra
- 2 tablespoons olive oil
- 2 teaspoons Cajun seasoning (store-bought or homemade)
- Salt to taste
- Lemon wedges, for serving (optional)

Instructions:

Preheat the Grill:
- Preheat your grill to medium-high heat.

Prepare the Okra:
- Rinse the okra under cold water and pat dry with paper towels.
- Trim the stems off the okra and cut them in half lengthwise.

Season the Okra:
- Place the okra halves in a large mixing bowl.
- Drizzle olive oil over the okra and toss to coat evenly.
- Sprinkle Cajun seasoning over the okra, tossing again to ensure that the okra is evenly coated with the seasoning.
- Season with salt to taste, if desired.

Grill the Okra:
- Arrange the seasoned okra halves on the preheated grill grate in a single layer, cut side down.
- Grill the okra for about 3-4 minutes on each side, or until they are tender and have grill marks.
- Be careful not to overcook the okra, as it can become mushy.

Serve:
- Once the okra is grilled to perfection, remove it from the grill and transfer it to a serving platter.
- Squeeze fresh lemon juice over the grilled okra, if desired, for an extra burst of flavor.
- Serve immediately as a delicious side dish or appetizer.

Enjoy:
- Enjoy the grilled okra with Cajun seasoning as a flavorful accompaniment to grilled meats, seafood, or as part of a vegetable platter.

Grilled okra with Cajun seasoning is a simple yet delicious way to enjoy this versatile vegetable. The smoky flavor from the grill and the spicy kick from the Cajun seasoning make it a perfect addition to any summer cookout or barbecue.

BBQ Chicken and Pineapple Skewers

Ingredients:

- 1 pound boneless, skinless chicken breasts or thighs, cut into bite-sized pieces
- 2 cups pineapple chunks, fresh or canned
- 1 bell pepper, cut into chunks
- 1 red onion, cut into chunks
- Wooden or metal skewers
- Salt and black pepper to taste
- BBQ sauce for brushing
- Chopped cilantro or parsley for garnish (optional)

Instructions:

Preheat the Grill:
- Preheat your grill to medium-high heat.

Prepare the Skewers:
- If using wooden skewers, soak them in water for at least 30 minutes to prevent them from burning on the grill.
- Thread the chicken pieces, pineapple chunks, bell pepper chunks, and red onion chunks onto the skewers, alternating between them. Leave a little space between each ingredient to ensure even cooking.

Season the Skewers:
- Season the skewers with salt and black pepper to taste.

Grill the Skewers:
- Place the assembled skewers on the preheated grill.
- Grill for about 8-10 minutes, turning occasionally, or until the chicken is cooked through and the vegetables are tender.
- During the last few minutes of grilling, brush the BBQ sauce generously over the skewers, turning them to coat evenly. Let the sauce caramelize slightly.

Serve:
- Once the skewers are done, remove them from the grill.
- Transfer the BBQ Chicken and Pineapple Skewers to a serving platter.
- Garnish with chopped cilantro or parsley, if desired.
- Serve hot and enjoy!

Variations:
- Feel free to customize the skewers by adding other vegetables such as cherry tomatoes, mushrooms, or zucchini.

- You can also marinate the chicken in your favorite BBQ sauce before threading it onto the skewers for extra flavor.

BBQ Chicken and Pineapple Skewers are perfect for summer cookouts, backyard BBQs, or weeknight dinners. They're easy to make and always a crowd-pleaser with their delicious combination of flavors. Enjoy!

Nashville Hot Chicken Sandwiches

Ingredients:

For the Nashville Hot Chicken:

- 4 boneless, skinless chicken breasts
- 1 cup buttermilk
- 1 cup all-purpose flour
- 1 tablespoon paprika
- 1 tablespoon garlic powder
- 1 tablespoon onion powder
- 1 tablespoon cayenne pepper (adjust to taste)
- Salt and black pepper to taste
- Vegetable oil for frying

For the Hot Chicken Sauce:

- 1/2 cup hot sauce (such as Louisiana-style hot sauce)
- 1/4 cup melted butter
- 2 tablespoons brown sugar
- 1 tablespoon paprika
- 1 tablespoon cayenne pepper
- 1 teaspoon garlic powder
- 1 teaspoon onion powder
- Salt to taste

For the Sandwiches:

- 4 sandwich buns
- Pickle slices
- Coleslaw (optional)
- Mayonnaise or ranch dressing (optional)
- Lettuce leaves (optional)
- Sliced tomatoes (optional)

Instructions:

    Prepare the Chicken:

- In a shallow dish, season the buttermilk with salt and black pepper to taste.
- Place the chicken breasts in the buttermilk mixture and let them marinate for at least 30 minutes, or up to overnight in the refrigerator.
- In another shallow dish, mix together the flour, paprika, garlic powder, onion powder, cayenne pepper, salt, and black pepper.
- Remove the chicken from the buttermilk mixture and dredge each piece in the seasoned flour, shaking off any excess.

Fry the Chicken:
- In a large skillet or deep fryer, heat vegetable oil to 350°F (175°C).
- Carefully add the chicken breasts to the hot oil and fry for about 6-8 minutes per side, or until golden brown and cooked through. The internal temperature should reach 165°F (74°C).
- Remove the fried chicken from the oil and place them on a wire rack or paper towels to drain excess oil.

Make the Hot Chicken Sauce:
- In a small saucepan, combine the hot sauce, melted butter, brown sugar, paprika, cayenne pepper, garlic powder, onion powder, and salt.
- Heat the sauce over medium heat, stirring occasionally, until the butter is melted and the ingredients are well combined.

Coat the Chicken in Hot Sauce:
- Once the fried chicken breasts have drained, brush or drizzle the hot chicken sauce over each piece, coating them generously.

Assemble the Sandwiches:
- Toast the sandwich buns if desired.
- Place a hot chicken breast on the bottom half of each bun.
- Top with pickle slices, coleslaw, mayonnaise or ranch dressing, lettuce leaves, sliced tomatoes, or any other desired toppings.
- Cover with the top half of the bun.

Serve:
- Serve the Nashville Hot Chicken Sandwiches immediately, and enjoy the spicy and flavorful goodness!

These Nashville Hot Chicken Sandwiches are sure to be a hit with anyone who loves a little heat. Adjust the level of spiciness to your preference by increasing or decreasing the amount of cayenne pepper in the hot chicken sauce. Enjoy!

Smoked Beef Short Ribs

Ingredients:

- 4-6 beef short ribs, bone-in (about 2-3 pounds)
- Salt and black pepper to taste
- Your favorite beef rub or seasoning blend
- Wood chips or chunks for smoking (such as hickory, oak, or cherry)

Instructions:

Prepare the Short Ribs:
- Trim any excess fat from the surface of the short ribs, leaving a thin layer for flavor and moisture.
- Season the short ribs generously with salt, black pepper, and your favorite beef rub or seasoning blend. Make sure to coat all sides evenly.

Prepare the Smoker:
- Preheat your smoker to 225°F (107°C). Use wood chips or chunks for smoking, soaking them in water for about 30 minutes before adding them to the smoker.

Smoke the Short Ribs:
- Once the smoker is preheated, place the seasoned beef short ribs directly on the smoker grate, bone side down.
- Close the lid and let the short ribs smoke for about 5-6 hours, maintaining a steady temperature of 225°F (107°C).

Check for Doneness:
- After 5-6 hours, check the internal temperature of the short ribs using a meat thermometer. They are done when the internal temperature reaches about 200-205°F (93-96°C) and the meat is tender and has pulled back from the bones.

Rest the Short Ribs:
- Once the short ribs are done, remove them from the smoker and wrap them tightly in aluminum foil.
- Let the wrapped short ribs rest for about 30-60 minutes. This allows the juices to redistribute, resulting in more tender and flavorful meat.

Serve:
- Unwrap the smoked beef short ribs and transfer them to a cutting board.
- Slice the short ribs between the bones and serve hot.
- Enjoy the delicious and smoky flavor of the smoked beef short ribs!

These smoked beef short ribs are sure to be a hit at your next barbecue gathering. Serve them with your favorite sides, such as coleslaw, baked beans, or potato salad, for a complete and satisfying meal.

Sweet Potato Casserole with Pecan Streusel Topping

Ingredients:

For the Sweet Potato Casserole:

- 4-5 medium sweet potatoes
- 1/2 cup granulated sugar
- 1/4 cup unsalted butter, melted
- 1/2 cup milk (or heavy cream for a richer texture)
- 2 large eggs, beaten
- 1 teaspoon vanilla extract
- 1/2 teaspoon ground cinnamon
- 1/4 teaspoon ground nutmeg
- 1/4 teaspoon salt

For the Pecan Streusel Topping:

- 1/2 cup all-purpose flour
- 1/2 cup packed brown sugar
- 1/4 cup cold unsalted butter, cut into small cubes
- 1/2 cup chopped pecans
- 1/2 teaspoon ground cinnamon
- Pinch of salt

Instructions:

Preheat the Oven:
- Preheat your oven to 375°F (190°C). Grease a 9x13-inch baking dish with butter or cooking spray.

Prepare the Sweet Potatoes:
- Peel the sweet potatoes and cut them into chunks.
- Place the sweet potato chunks in a large pot of boiling water and cook until fork-tender, about 15-20 minutes.
- Drain the sweet potatoes and transfer them to a large mixing bowl.

Mash the Sweet Potatoes:
- Mash the cooked sweet potatoes using a potato masher or fork until smooth and creamy.

Make the Sweet Potato Mixture:

- To the mashed sweet potatoes, add the granulated sugar, melted butter, milk, beaten eggs, vanilla extract, ground cinnamon, ground nutmeg, and salt.
- Stir until all the ingredients are well combined and the mixture is smooth.

Transfer to Baking Dish:
- Spread the sweet potato mixture evenly into the prepared baking dish, smoothing the top with a spatula.

Make the Pecan Streusel Topping:
- In a medium mixing bowl, combine the all-purpose flour, brown sugar, cold cubed butter, chopped pecans, ground cinnamon, and a pinch of salt.
- Use a pastry cutter or your fingers to blend the ingredients together until the mixture resembles coarse crumbs.

Add the Topping:
- Sprinkle the pecan streusel topping evenly over the sweet potato mixture in the baking dish.

Bake:
- Place the baking dish in the preheated oven and bake for 25-30 minutes, or until the topping is golden brown and the sweet potato mixture is set.

Serve:
- Remove the sweet potato casserole from the oven and let it cool slightly before serving.
- Serve warm and enjoy!

This Sweet Potato Casserole with Pecan Streusel Topping is a delicious and comforting side dish that pairs well with roasted turkey, ham, or any other main course. It's sure to be a hit at your next holiday feast or family gathering!

Cajun BBQ Shrimp and Grits

Ingredients:

For the Caju n BBQ Shrimp:

- 1 pound large shrimp, peeled and deveined
- 2 tablespoons Cajun seasoning
- 2 tablespoons olive oil
- 2 cloves garlic, minced
- 1/4 cup barbecue sauce
- 2 tablespoons Worcestershire sauce
- 1 tablespoon lemon juice
- Salt and black pepper to taste
- Chopped fresh parsley for garnish (optional)

For the Grits:

- 1 cup stone-ground grits
- 4 cups water or chicken broth
- 1 cup shredded cheddar cheese
- 2 tablespoons unsalted butter
- Salt and black pepper to taste

Instructions:

Prepare the Grits:
- In a medium saucepan, bring the water or chicken broth to a boil.
- Gradually whisk in the stone-ground grits, stirring constantly to prevent lumps.
- Reduce the heat to low and simmer, stirring occasionally, for about 20-25 minutes, or until the grits are thick and creamy.
- Stir in the shredded cheddar cheese and butter until melted and well combined.
- Season with salt and black pepper to taste. Keep warm while you prepare the shrimp.

Prepare the Cajun BBQ Shrimp:
- In a large bowl, toss the peeled and deveined shrimp with Cajun seasoning until evenly coated.

- Heat the olive oil in a large skillet over medium-high heat.
- Add the minced garlic to the skillet and sauté for about 1 minute, until fragrant.
- Add the seasoned shrimp to the skillet and cook for 2-3 minutes per side, or until they turn pink and opaque.
- Stir in the barbecue sauce, Worcestershire sauce, and lemon juice, tossing the shrimp to coat evenly.
- Season with salt and black pepper to taste.

Serve:
- Divide the creamy grits among serving bowls.
- Spoon the Cajun BBQ shrimp and sauce over the grits.
- Garnish with chopped fresh parsley, if desired.
- Serve immediately and enjoy!

This Cajun BBQ Shrimp and Grits recipe is sure to impress with its bold flavors and comforting textures. It's perfect for brunch, lunch, or dinner, and will quickly become a favorite in your recipe collection!

Grilled Asparagus with Lemon-Herb Butter

Ingredients:

- 1 bunch of fresh asparagus spears, tough ends trimmed
- 2 tablespoons olive oil
- Salt and black pepper to taste

For the Lemon-Herb Butter:

- 4 tablespoons unsalted butter, softened
- Zest of 1 lemon
- 1 tablespoon freshly squeezed lemon juice
- 2 cloves garlic, minced
- 1 tablespoon chopped fresh parsley
- 1 tablespoon chopped fresh chives (or green onions)
- Salt and black pepper to taste

Instructions:

Prepare the Lemon-Herb Butter:
- In a small bowl, combine the softened butter, lemon zest, lemon juice, minced garlic, chopped parsley, and chopped chives.
- Season with salt and black pepper to taste.
- Mix until well combined. Set aside.

Prepare the Asparagus:
- Preheat your grill to medium-high heat.
- Place the trimmed asparagus spears on a baking sheet.
- Drizzle the olive oil over the asparagus, then season with salt and black pepper. Toss the asparagus to coat evenly.

Grill the Asparagus:
- Place the seasoned asparagus spears directly on the preheated grill.
- Grill for about 5-7 minutes, turning occasionally, or until the asparagus is tender and lightly charred.

Serve:
- Once the asparagus is grilled to your desired level of doneness, transfer it to a serving platter.
- Dollop the lemon-herb butter over the grilled asparagus while it's still hot, allowing it to melt slightly.

- Garnish with additional chopped parsley or chives, if desired.
- Serve immediately and enjoy!

This Grilled Asparagus with Lemon-Herb Butter is bursting with fresh flavors and makes a wonderful addition to any summer meal. It's quick and easy to prepare, yet impressive enough to serve to guests at your next barbecue or cookout. Enjoy!

BBQ Pulled Pork Stuffed Sweet Potatoes

Ingredients:

For the BBQ Pulled Pork:

- 2 pounds pork shoulder (also known as pork butt), trimmed of excess fat
- Salt and black pepper to taste
- 1 tablespoon olive oil
- 1 onion, diced
- 3 cloves garlic, minced
- 1 cup barbecue sauce (your favorite variety)
- 1 cup chicken or beef broth
- 2 tablespoons brown sugar
- 1 tablespoon apple cider vinegar
- 1 teaspoon smoked paprika
- 1/2 teaspoon cayenne pepper (optional, for heat)

For the Sweet Potatoes:

- 4 large sweet potatoes
- Olive oil for brushing
- Salt and black pepper to taste

Instructions:

Prepare the BBQ Pulled Pork:
- Preheat your oven to 325°F (165°C).
- Season the pork shoulder generously with salt and black pepper.
- Heat olive oil in a large oven-safe pot or Dutch oven over medium-high heat.
- Sear the pork shoulder on all sides until browned, then remove from the pot and set aside.
- In the same pot, add diced onion and minced garlic. Sauté until softened and fragrant.
- Return the seared pork shoulder to the pot.
- In a mixing bowl, combine barbecue sauce, chicken or beef broth, brown sugar, apple cider vinegar, smoked paprika, and cayenne pepper. Pour the mixture over the pork shoulder.
- Cover the pot with a lid and transfer it to the preheated oven.

- Bake for 3-4 hours, or until the pork is fork-tender and easily pulls apart.
- Remove the pork from the oven and shred it using two forks. Stir the shredded pork in the cooking liquid to coat it evenly. Set aside.

Prepare the Sweet Potatoes:
- Preheat your grill to medium-high heat.
- Wash and scrub the sweet potatoes thoroughly under cold water.
- Pierce the sweet potatoes several times with a fork to create steam vents.
- Brush the sweet potatoes with olive oil and season with salt and black pepper.
- Wrap each sweet potato individually in aluminum foil.

Grill the Sweet Potatoes:
- Place the foil-wrapped sweet potatoes on the preheated grill.
- Grill for 45-60 minutes, or until the sweet potatoes are tender when pierced with a fork. Cooking time may vary depending on the size and thickness of the sweet potatoes.

Assemble the Stuffed Sweet Potatoes:
- Remove the grilled sweet potatoes from the grill and carefully unwrap them from the foil.
- Slice each sweet potato lengthwise down the center, without cutting all the way through.
- Fluff the insides of the sweet potatoes with a fork.
- Spoon a generous amount of BBQ pulled pork into the center of each sweet potato.

Serve:
- Serve the BBQ Pulled Pork Stuffed Sweet Potatoes hot.
- Optionally, garnish with chopped fresh parsley or green onions.
- Enjoy!

These BBQ Pulled Pork Stuffed Sweet Potatoes are a hearty and flavorful meal that's perfect for any occasion. They're sure to be a hit with family and friends!

Smoked Chicken Thighs with Alabama White Sauce

Ingredients:

For the Smoked Chicken Thighs:

- 8 bone-in, skin-on chicken thighs
- Salt and black pepper to taste
- Your favorite chicken rub or seasoning blend
- Wood chips or chunks for smoking (such as hickory, apple, or oak)

For the Alabama White Sauce:

- 1 cup mayonnaise
- 1/4 cup apple cider vinegar
- 2 tablespoons prepared horseradish
- 1 tablespoon Dijon mustard
- 1 tablespoon lemon juice
- 1 teaspoon Worcestershire sauce
- 1 clove garlic, minced
- 1/2 teaspoon black pepper
- 1/2 teaspoon salt
- 1/2 teaspoon smoked paprika
- 1/4 teaspoon cayenne pepper (optional, for heat)

Instructions:

Prepare the Chicken Thighs:
- Rinse the chicken thighs under cold water and pat them dry with paper towels.
- Season the chicken thighs generously with salt, black pepper, and your favorite chicken rub or seasoning blend. Make sure to coat all sides evenly.
- Let the seasoned chicken thighs sit at room temperature for about 30 minutes while you prepare the smoker.

Preheat the Smoker:
- Preheat your smoker to 250°F (120°C). Use wood chips or chunks for smoking, soaking them in water for about 30 minutes before adding them to the smoker.

Smoke the Chicken Thighs:

- Once the smoker is preheated, place the seasoned chicken thighs directly on the smoker grate, skin side up.
- Close the lid and let the chicken thighs smoke for about 2-3 hours, or until they reach an internal temperature of 165°F (74°C) and the skin is golden brown and crispy.

Prepare the Alabama White Sauce:
- In a medium mixing bowl, whisk together the mayonnaise, apple cider vinegar, prepared horseradish, Dijon mustard, lemon juice, Worcestershire sauce, minced garlic, black pepper, salt, smoked paprika, and cayenne pepper (if using).
- Taste the sauce and adjust the seasoning according to your preference. Add more salt, pepper, or other seasonings as needed.

Serve:
- Once the smoked chicken thighs are done, remove them from the smoker and let them rest for a few minutes.
- Serve the smoked chicken thighs hot, with the Alabama white sauce on the side for dipping or drizzling.
- Enjoy the delicious combination of smoky chicken thighs and tangy Alabama white sauce!

This smoked chicken thighs with Alabama white sauce recipe is sure to be a hit at your next barbecue or cookout. The flavorful chicken paired with the creamy and tangy sauce creates a mouthwatering dish that everyone will love.

Southern BBQ Baked Macaroni and Cheese

Ingredients:

- 1 pound elbow macaroni
- 1/2 cup unsalted butter
- 1/2 cup all-purpose flour
- 4 cups whole milk
- 4 cups shredded sharp cheddar cheese
- 1 cup shredded smoked gouda cheese
- 1 cup shredded mozzarella cheese
- 1 cup barbecue sauce (your favorite variety)
- Salt and black pepper to taste
- 1/2 teaspoon smoked paprika
- 1/2 cup breadcrumbs (optional, for topping)
- Chopped fresh parsley for garnish (optional)

Instructions:

Preheat the Oven:
- Preheat your oven to 350°F (175°C). Grease a 9x13-inch baking dish with butter or cooking spray.

Cook the Macaroni:
- Cook the elbow macaroni according to the package instructions in a large pot of salted boiling water until al dente. Drain and set aside.

Make the Cheese Sauce:
- In a large saucepan, melt the unsalted butter over medium heat.
- Stir in the all-purpose flour and cook, stirring constantly, for 1-2 minutes to make a roux.
- Gradually whisk in the whole milk, stirring constantly to prevent lumps from forming.
- Cook the sauce, stirring frequently, until it thickens and coats the back of a spoon, about 5-7 minutes.
- Reduce the heat to low and gradually stir in the shredded sharp cheddar cheese, shredded smoked gouda cheese, and shredded mozzarella cheese until melted and smooth.
- Stir in the barbecue sauce until well combined.
- Season the cheese sauce with salt, black pepper, and smoked paprika to taste.

Combine the Macaroni and Cheese Sauce:

- In a large mixing bowl, combine the cooked elbow macaroni and the prepared cheese sauce. Stir until the macaroni is evenly coated with the sauce.

Bake the Macaroni and Cheese:
- Transfer the macaroni and cheese mixture to the prepared baking dish, spreading it out evenly.
- If desired, sprinkle breadcrumbs over the top for added crunch.
- Bake in the preheated oven for 25-30 minutes, or until the top is golden brown and the cheese is bubbly and gooey.

Serve:
- Remove the Southern BBQ Baked Macaroni and Cheese from the oven and let it cool for a few minutes.
- Garnish with chopped fresh parsley, if desired.
- Serve hot and enjoy the delicious and indulgent flavors!

This Southern BBQ Baked Macaroni and Cheese is sure to be a hit at any gathering or family dinner. The creamy cheese sauce infused with barbecue flavor takes this classic comfort food to a whole new level of deliciousness!

Grilled Artichokes with Garlic-Herb Butter

Ingredients:

For the Grilled Artichokes:

- 2 large artichokes
- 1 lemon, halved
- Olive oil
- Salt and black pepper to taste

For the Garlic-Herb Butter:

- 1/2 cup unsalted butter, softened
- 2 cloves garlic, minced
- 2 tablespoons chopped fresh parsley
- 1 tablespoon chopped fresh thyme
- 1 tablespoon chopped fresh rosemary
- Salt and black pepper to taste

Instructions:

Prepare the Artichokes:
- Fill a large bowl with cold water and squeeze the lemon halves into the water.
- Trim the stem of each artichoke to create a flat base. Using kitchen shears, trim the top inch of each artichoke to remove the sharp tips from the leaves.
- Cut the artichokes in half lengthwise.
- Use a spoon to scoop out the fuzzy choke from the center of each artichoke half.
- Place the trimmed artichoke halves in the bowl of lemon water to prevent them from browning.

Parboil the Artichokes:
- Fill a large pot with water and bring it to a boil over high heat.
- Once the water is boiling, add the artichoke halves.
- Cook the artichokes for 10-15 minutes, or until they are slightly tender when pierced with a fork.
- Drain the artichokes and pat them dry with paper towels.

Prepare the Garlic-Herb Butter:
- In a small bowl, combine the softened butter, minced garlic, chopped parsley, chopped thyme, chopped rosemary, salt, and black pepper. Mix until well combined.

Grill the Artichokes:
- Preheat your grill to medium-high heat.
- Brush the parboiled artichoke halves with olive oil and season them with salt and black pepper.
- Place the artichokes on the preheated grill, cut side down.
- Grill the artichokes for 5-7 minutes, or until they are lightly charred and tender.

Serve:
- Remove the grilled artichokes from the grill and transfer them to a serving platter.
- Serve the artichokes hot, with the garlic-herb butter on the side for dipping.
- Enjoy the delicious and flavorful grilled artichokes with garlic-herb butter!

These grilled artichokes with garlic-herb butter are sure to be a hit at your next cookout or gathering. They make a fantastic appetizer or side dish that's both elegant and delicious.

Bourbon BBQ Glazed Pork Tenderloin

Ingredients:

For the Pork Tenderloin:

- 2 pork tenderloins, about 1-1.5 pounds each
- Salt and black pepper to taste
- Olive oil for searing

For the Bourbon BBQ Glaze:

- 1/2 cup bourbon whiskey
- 1/2 cup barbecue sauce
- 2 tablespoons brown sugar
- 2 tablespoons soy sauce
- 2 cloves garlic, minced
- 1 teaspoon Dijon mustard
- 1/2 teaspoon smoked paprika
- Salt and black pepper to taste

Instructions:

Prepare the Pork Tenderloin:
- Preheat your oven to 375°F (190°C).
- Pat the pork tenderloins dry with paper towels.
- Season them generously with salt and black pepper.

Sear the Pork Tenderloin:
- Heat a large oven-safe skillet over medium-high heat.
- Add a drizzle of olive oil to the skillet.
- Once the skillet is hot, sear the pork tenderloins on all sides until golden brown, about 2-3 minutes per side.

Make the Bourbon BBQ Glaze:
- In a small saucepan, combine the bourbon whiskey, barbecue sauce, brown sugar, soy sauce, minced garlic, Dijon mustard, smoked paprika, salt, and black pepper.
- Stir well to combine.
- Place the saucepan over medium heat and bring the mixture to a simmer.

- Let it simmer for about 5-7 minutes, stirring occasionally, until the sauce has thickened slightly.

Glaze the Pork Tenderloin:
- Brush the bourbon BBQ glaze generously over the seared pork tenderloins, reserving some glaze for basting.
- Place the skillet with the glazed pork tenderloins in the preheated oven.

Bake the Pork Tenderloin:
- Bake the pork tenderloins in the oven for about 15-20 minutes, or until they reach an internal temperature of 145°F (63°C), measured with a meat thermometer.
- Baste the pork tenderloins with additional glaze halfway through the cooking time.

Rest and Serve:
- Once the pork tenderloins are done, remove them from the oven and let them rest for 5-10 minutes before slicing.
- Slice the pork tenderloins into medallions and serve hot, drizzling any remaining glaze over the top.
- Enjoy the succulent and flavorful Bourbon BBQ Glazed Pork Tenderloin!

This Bourbon BBQ Glazed Pork Tenderloin is perfect for a special dinner or entertaining guests. Serve it with your favorite side dishes, such as roasted vegetables, mashed potatoes, or a crisp salad, for a delicious and satisfying meal.

BBQ Pulled Jackfruit Sandwiches (for a vegetarian option)

Ingredients:

For the BBQ Pulled Jackfruit:

- 2 cans (20 ounces each) young green jackfruit in brine or water, drained and rinsed
- 1 tablespoon olive oil
- 1 onion, finely chopped
- 3 cloves garlic, minced
- 1 cup barbecue sauce
- 1/2 cup vegetable broth or water
- 2 tablespoons tomato paste
- 1 tablespoon apple cider vinegar
- 1 tablespoon brown sugar or maple syrup
- 1 teaspoon smoked paprika
- 1/2 teaspoon cumin
- Salt and pepper to taste

For Serving:

- Burger buns or sandwich rolls
- Coleslaw (optional, for topping)
- Pickles (optional, for topping)

Instructions:

Prepare the Jackfruit:
- Rinse the canned jackfruit under cold water to remove any brine or canning liquid. Pat the jackfruit dry with paper towels.
- Using your hands or a fork, shred the jackfruit into smaller pieces, resembling pulled pork. Discard any large seeds or tough core pieces.

Cook the BBQ Pulled Jackfruit:
- Heat olive oil in a large skillet or pot over medium heat.
- Add chopped onion and minced garlic to the skillet. Sauté for 2-3 minutes until softened and fragrant.
- Add the shredded jackfruit to the skillet and cook for 5-7 minutes, stirring occasionally, until lightly browned.

- In a small bowl, whisk together barbecue sauce, vegetable broth or water, tomato paste, apple cider vinegar, brown sugar or maple syrup, smoked paprika, cumin, salt, and pepper.
- Pour the barbecue sauce mixture over the jackfruit in the skillet. Stir to combine.
- Reduce the heat to low, cover, and let the jackfruit simmer for 20-25 minutes, stirring occasionally, until the sauce has thickened and the jackfruit is tender.

Assemble the Sandwiches:
- Toast the burger buns or sandwich rolls if desired.
- Spoon a generous amount of BBQ pulled jackfruit onto the bottom half of each bun.
- Top with coleslaw and pickles, if using.
- Place the top half of the bun over the filling to form a sandwich.

Serve:
- Serve the BBQ Pulled Jackfruit Sandwiches immediately.
- Enjoy the delicious vegetarian alternative to pulled pork sandwiches!

These BBQ Pulled Jackfruit Sandwiches are flavorful, satisfying, and perfect for vegetarians or anyone looking to enjoy a meatless meal. They're great for gatherings, parties, or weeknight dinners.